Texas?

What Do You Know About
the Lone Star State?

Archie P. McDonald

Texas Christian University Press

FORT WORTH

Library of Congress Cataloging-in-Publication Data

McDonald, Archie P.
    Texas? : what do you know about the Lone Star State? / by
Archie P. McDonald.
      p.   cm.
    ISBN 0-87565-120-8
    1. Texas—Miscellanea.   I. Title.
F386.M348   1993
976.4—dc20
                                          93-14665
                                            CIP
                                            AC

Drawings: Charles Shaw
Cover: painted photograph by Cheryl Long
Design: Barbara Whitehead

Contents

For Judy
She Makes Texas A Better Place

Acknowledgments

Books are cooperative efforts, and when a person gets to put his name on one as the individual who primarily is responsible for it occupying space in book stores, there is a sort of a protocol that he "acknowledge" all the kind folks who helped along the way. I am going to do that. Protocol or not, I owe some debts.

First, the inspiration for this book came from Jaime O'Neill, whose *What Do You Know? The Ultimate Test of Common (And Not So Common) Knowledge* pioneered the field. O'Neill must be the kind of teacher we wish taught our children. His chagrin at discovering significant gaps in the previous education of his students did not make him simply accept the circumstance; he sought a way to solve the problem. We first corresponded after I saw him on CBS's "60 Minutes" with Mike Wallace, and we began to exchange tests and test results. Jaime was the first to encourage me to do a similar book on Texas.

Second, I want to thank Vartan Gregorian and Jim

Veninga. Although I was only a member of a large audience when Gregorian spoke to a conference of state humanities council members, his talk had a significant influence upon my thinking about what should be a part of everyone's education. Though we did not meet personally, his tracks can be found in this book, especially in "Gregorian's Game." Jim Veninga, long-time director of the Texas Committee for the Humanities, is the kind of person I admire. Both Gregorian and Veninga light candles against the darkness.

Thanks also to all the folks who compiled the *Handbook of Texas*, one of the primary sources for the questions (and the answers) that appear in this book. Also the following, whose various works provided me with needed data: Mike Kingston for the *Texas Almanac*; Ray Stephens and William Holmes for *Historical Atlas of Texas*; Don Graham for *Cowboys and Cadillacs: How Hollywood Looks at Texas*; Francis Edward Abernethy for *Singin' Texas* and for just being Ab; the compilers of *Waltz Across Texas Plus 12 Lone Star Giants* and of *Texas Centennial Song Book*; A. C. Greene for *The 50 Best Books On Texas*; Jim Pohl for—as they say in television—being "on sports"; and Rupert Richardson, Ernest Wallace, Adrian Anderson, Seymour V. ("Ike") Connor, Robert A. Calvert, Arnoldo De Leon, and Ted Fehrenbach, all of whom have educated me about Texas.

Appreciation is expressed to Linda Brown, who corrected my typing mistakes, Catherine Hull, who helped with manuscript preparation, and Elizabeth Huff, who became a regular at the library to check on things I was too lazy to verify for myself.

I wish to acknowledge all the teachers who helped me appreciate and learn to love the history of Texas and of

Acknowledgments

the United States, beginning with my seventh-grade teacher, Mrs. Henrich, and continuing through Bob Warren, Merrill Rippy, Preston Williams, Ralph Wooster, Frank Vandiver, and T. Harry Williams; and teachers of another sort, including Ben Procter, Max Lale, Haskell Monroe, F. Lee Lawrence, J. P. Bryan, Glenn McCutchen, Kent Biffle, William J. Brophy, James V. Reese, R. G. Dean, Jenkins Garrett, Clifton Caldwell, Hans Mark, and Jim Michener. Each helped me grow.

Introduction

From early in the 1980s until the end of the Sesquicentennial celebration in 1986, Texans nearly drowned in the Niagara of their past. Communities that had neglected their own history, or its role in the larger mosaic of the state, awoke to the fact that Texas as a definable entity had reached 150 years of age; cities that had honored and preserved their history all along kicked into high gear.

For one who had worked in the vineyard of Texas history for two decades, the Sesquicentennial brought problems and opportunities. I was asked to write a complete history of Texas for the *Dallas Times Herald* that appeared on March 7, 1982. I was told that distribution reached several hundred thousand. It didn't matter that March 8 found my writing lining bird cages; that is possibly the largest single distribution of a history of Texas to its time. I know and appreciate that a number of people read it because they wrote to question facts, correct mistakes, and disagree with interpretations.

Later, the supplement was published in book form under the title *Texas: All Hail The Mighty State.*

Two other responsibilities led to more writing and many speeches during the mid-1980s. First, I served on the state Sesquicentennial Commission and, second, I had the privilege of serving as president of the Texas State Historical Association for 1985–1986. Invitations for too many speaking engagements followed the appointments and I logged nearly 30,000 air and highway miles during the year.

Reflecting on it later convinced me that visits with my fellow Texans renewed my commitment to speaking and writing primarily for the lay historian, the citizen who works in a bank or is a stockbroker, a car salesman or factory worker—any Texan who is interested in the heritage of our state and our nation. Long ago I accepted the fact that my fellow professional historians know what I know and more. My challenge was to reach everyone with the message that a basic knowledge of Texas history was important.

My link with TSHA required that I make the presidential address to an assembled membership at the annual meeting in Austin. Everyone who is called upon to make such a speech feels inadequate to the task, and most review what their predecessors have done to avoid duplication and to search for ideas. What could I contribute? What could I pass on to my successors? I decided I would challenge the membership—both professional and lay historians. What I determined to do was to call the members' attention to a deplorable, but correctable, trouble in our state and in the rest of the nation: historical amnesia, or, in the words of educator and humanist Vartan Gregorian, "living in a perpetual present." Gregorian's thesis seems impossible; sadly, it is not.

Texans, I found, are up to the top of their cowboy boots in this historical amnesia. When preparing my talk for the Texas State Historical Association, I asked colleagues to administer a quiz to friends, students, colleagues, family—anyone who was game to show their knowledge of Texas history. The majority should have been able to score at least fifty percent just because they lived and functioned in Texas. Sadly, that was not the case.

I admit that many of the questions might have been answered only after taking a course in Texas history or a little more than average study. But how about these? Only fifty-one percent—about half the Texans taking the quiz, whose ancestors vowed to "Remember The Alamo"—could name the battle where Santa Anna defeated Texas forces on March 6, 1836; thirty-three percent accurately identified the Battle of San Jacinto as the turning point of the Revolution; and forty-four percent—less than half—knew that Sam Houston was the first elected president of the Republic. Seven percent knew that M. B. Lamar was the president who offered a radically different program from Houston's, and just five percent knew the name of the first governor of Texas.

Eighty-three percent did not know the name of the first native-born Texan to become president of the United States, and fifty-seven percent could not name the Texan who became president after John F. Kennedy was assassinated in Dallas on November 22, 1963. Over half did know how many United States senators represent Texas, but half of those who did could not name both, and some could not name either.

Geographic amnesia was prevalent as well. Only about half could name all three rivers that help form Texas' borders, and only about two-thirds could name the four contiguous states of the union that surround the Lone Star State.

Over half did not know the title of the state song (I would be afraid to ask how many knew the words or the tune), but three-quarters could name the state bird and state flower. And—when this sample was taken in 1985—only sixty-five percent knew the meaning of the term "sesquicentennial."

Some of the responses cannot help but amuse. Someone thought that the first humans in Texas were the Pilgrims; another that Columbus or Leonardo da Vinci led the search in Texas for the seven cities of gold; that George Washington was Texas' first *empresario;* that David Crockett was the most significant *empresario;* that Texas Independence Day was July 4; that Santa Anna defeated the Texans at Gettysburg; that Bunker Hill was the turning point of the Texas Revolution; that Daniel Boone was the first president of the Texas Republic; that the Rough Riders, the F.B.I., the Lone Ranger, or John Wayne was the state's legendary law enforcement agency; or that Ima Hogg or Ladybird Johnson was our only (to 1985) woman governor.

Some thought that Abraham Lincoln was the first native-born Texan to become president; that the state is bordered by the Arkansas, Mississippi, Colorado, Pecos, Trinity, or Nile rivers and by the states of Arizona, Alabama, Colorado, California, Montana, Nevada, Georgia, Ohio, or North Dakota; that the Grand Canyon is part of Texas; that we have fifteen United States senators; that John Tower was then the governor; that the state song is "The Yellow Rose of Texas," "Deep In

The Heart Of Texas," or "The Eyes of Texas"; that the state bird is the bluebird, the eagle, the bluejay, the redbird, or the roadrunner; that the state flower is the rose; that we had once been a part of France, Germany, Italy, Europe, Louisiana, or South America; or, finally, that "sesquicentennial" is Latin for "Lone Star."

Vartan Gregorian dared his listeners to imagine that only one had survived a nuclear holocaust or some similar disaster. He suggested that all libraries, museums, books, oral history tapes and video records have been destroyed; that there is no record of the past except the knowledge of the sole survivor.

Applying his game to a Texas scenario, the loner is a Texan and the proud possessor of a college diploma, perhaps even advanced degrees. He or she is an educated person and the only survivor of the state's education process. Space aliens descend on the last Lone Star stater and ask: "How does the Texas economy work? How do you 'make' oil? You appear to have had many museums—which were your best and in what did each specialize, if anything? If Texas has hosted writers, painters, composers, or other artists, identify them and explain their work. Did Texans pioneer any medical or other humanitarian work? Did your society support games of sport or produce significant athletes? Did the scientific community produce important technology— and what was the name of that fellow in Dallas who worked with silicone? Did Texas have significant women, black, or Hispanic leaders? Finally, just what *does* 'Sesquicentennial' mean?"

The questions could go on and on: too much information wanted, too little of it retained.

Test yourself in the pages that follow. Just what do you know about the Lone Star State?

Sources of the Questions
and Answers

Since this book is intended to convince doubters of the value of *reading* about Texas so they will *know* about Texas, it is only reasonable to indicate some of the best sources for doing just that.

One of the most useful—perhaps the foremost compendium on the history of Texas—is the multi-volume *Handbook of Texas*. First published in 1952 under the general editorship of Walter Prescott Webb in a two-volume format, and supplemented with a third volume edited by Eldon Branda and L. Tuffly Ellis in 1976, this collection contains more data about Texas than any other. Any serious student of Texas history and life ought to own a set; almost everyone else in Texas ought to know about it. For the past decade or more its publisher, the Texas State Historical Association, has invested many dollars and many research hours in preparing a revision and expansion. The updated edition, due out in 1995, will contain six volumes.

Right behind the *Handbook* is the venerable *Texas Almanac*, published more or less continuously since 1857 by the *Dallas Morning News* and its parent company, and for the last several years prepared by Mike Kingston. It is largely a compilation of statistics, but does contain interesting essays in each volume. It now appears biennially.

For the geography of Texas, in addition to articles in the *Handbook*, the *Historical Atlas of Texas*, prepared by A. Ray Stephens and William M. Holmes (Norman: University of Oklahoma Press, 1989) is useful. This volume contains sixty-four maps of Texas structured to show both physical and cultural geography, each with an explanatory essay on the opposing page. Also useful is the "Texas Official Highway Travel Map," available free from the Texas Department of Transportation.

For questions on cultural matters, the following proved most useful. *Cowboys and Cadillacs: How Hollywood Looks At Texas*, by Don Graham (Austin: Texas Monthly Press, 1983), is a good review of films about Texas and Texans. For music, *Singin' Texas* by Francis Edward Abernethy, with music by Dan Beaty (Dallas: E-Heart Press, 1983) is helpful; as are *Waltz Across Texas Plus 12 Lone Star Giants*, edited by Carol Cuellar and Ed Thornton (Hialeah, Florida: Columbia Pictures Publications, 1981) and *Texas Centennial Song Book*, Sesquicentennial Edition, originally printed in 1936 and reprinted in 1986 (Dallas: Turner Company). For literature, *The 50 Best Books On Texas*, by A. C. Greene (Dallas: Pressworks Publishing, 1982) is both fun and profitable.

My best recommendation for reading on Texas sports is James W. Pohl's chapter "Sports in Texas," *Texas Heritage*, second edition, edited by Ben Procter and

Archie P. McDonald (Arlington Heights, Illinois: Harlan Davidson, 1991), and Bill O'Neal, *The Texas League* (Austin: Eakin Press, 1987).

Many answers to the questions that follow can be found in general sources—some scholarly, some less so. The standard *Texas: The Lone Star State,* by Rupert N. Richardson, Ernest Wallace, and Adrian Anderson (Englewood Cliffs, New Jersey: Prentice-Hall, 1943, and revised frequently since then) is a good place to start. See also *Texas: A History,* by Seymour V. Connor (New York: Thomas Y. Crowell, 1971). Possibly *the* best book for twentieth-century Texas history is *The History of Texas* by Robert A. Calvert and Arnoldo De Leon (Arlington Heights, Illinois: Harlan Davidson, 1990). Personally, I enjoy T. R. Fehrenbach's *Lone Star: A History of Texas and The Texans* (New York: Macmillan, 1968). Finally, immodesty compels me to mention my own *Texas: All Hail The Mighty State,* written as a supplement to the *Dallas Times Herald* for the Sesquicentennial. It was republished by Eakin Press of Austin in 1983 and revised in 1991.

1

Texas History

"Diagnostic Quiz"

This test is to determine what you know about general topics, and there will be no final grade. Don't cheat for that would deprive you of the joy of knowing what you know. Relax and let the questions take you through a mini-course in Texas history, government, and geography. Read through the questions, and don't call out for someone to come and help you—it will be more fun to ask others the questions after you have looked up the answers you didn't know.

The Quiz

1. What term identifies the first humans who inhabited what was later known as Texas? _____

2. The Spaniard who led the largest exploration from New Spain into Texas in 1540 was? _____

3. The French explorer who founded Fort St. Louis was? _____

4. Established in 1718, the great half-way mission in Texas, situated on a river, was? _____

5. The first person who obtained permission to settle American colonists in Texas was? _____

6. The most significant *empresario* and colonizer in Texas was? _____

7. Texas independence day is? _____

8. Santa Anna defeated Texas forces on March 6, 1836, at what battle? _____

9. The battle of the Texas Revolution that proved to be its turning point was? _____

10. The first elected president of the Texas Republic was? _____

11. The president who advocated an expansive policy for the Republic of Texas was? _____

12. The first governor of Texas was? _____

13. Texas' first, and until 1979, only Republican governor, was? _____

14. Texas' legendary law enforcement agency was (is)?
    _____

15. The Texas constitution was adopted in what year?
    _____

16. Texas' most progressive governor, who fought to establish the Railroad Commission, was? _____
    _____

17. Which is older, the University of Texas at Austin or Texas A&M University? _____

18. Texas' only governor to be impeached and removed from office was? _____

19. Who was the first governor to receive a college degree? _____

20. Texas first woman governor was? _____

21. The first person born in Texas who became president of the United States was? _____

22. The most decorated soldier of World War II, a Texan, was? _____

23. The Texas governor who bolted the Democratic Party in 1952 was? _____

24. The Texan who became president on November 22, 1963, was? _____

25. Which three rivers help form Texas boundaries?
_____

26. _____
27. _____

28. What four of the United States border Texas? _____
_____

29. _____
30. _____
31. _____

32. What is Texas' largest city? _____

33. How many U. S. senators represent Texas in Washington? _____

34. How often does the Texas legislature meet in regular session? _____

35. What is the state song of Texas? _____

36. What is the state bird of Texas? _____

37. What is the state flower of Texas? _____

38. What is the state tree of Texas? _____

39. How many counties does Texas have? _____

40. Texas has been a part of what four countries? _____
_____

41. _____

42. _____

43. _____

44. Who is the current lieutenant governor of Texas?
_____

45. Who is the current governor of Texas? _____

Answers

1. Paleo-Americans.
2. Francisco Vásquez de Coronado.
3. Rene Robert Cavelier, Sieur de La Salle.
4. San Antonio de Valero Mission (also known as San Antonio de Padua Mission and later as the Alamo).
5. Moses Austin.
6. Stephen Fuller Austin.
7. March 2.
8. The Battle of the Alamo (the final assault on March 6, 1836 ended a thirteen-day siege of the fortress).
9. The Battle of San Jacinto, April 20–21, 1836 (the major action occurred on the afternoon of April 21, 1836).
10. Sam Houston.
11. Mirabeau Buonaparte Lamar.
12. James Pinckney Henderson.
13. Edmund J. Davis.
14. The Texas Rangers.
15. 1876 (the constitution was written by the Convention of 1875 and adopted by an election held in February 1876).
16. James Stephen Hogg.
17. Texas A&M (founded in 1876; The University of Texas was established in 1883).
18. James E. Ferguson.
19. Pat Neff.
20. Mrs. Miriam Amanda Ferguson.
21. Dwight David Eisenhower.
22. Audie Murphy.
23. Allan Shivers.
24. Lyndon Baines Johnson.

25. Rio Grande.
26. Sabine River.
27. Red River.
28. Louisiana.
29. Arkansas.
30. Oklahoma.
31. New Mexico.
32. Houston.
33. Two.
34. Every other year in odd-numbered years (even-numbered years are when elections are held).
35. "Texas, Our Texas."
36. Mockingbird.
37. Bluebonnet.
38. Pecan.
39. 254.
40. Spain.
41. Mexico.
42. The United States.
43. The Confederate States of America.
44. Bob Bullock (1991–).
45. Ann Richards (1991–).

2

Where Are We?

Many Texans don't know much about the geography of their state—plain and simple geography. We hurry eastward on Interstate 10, crossing important rivers between Houston and the Louisiana border. In the way of modern bridge building, we can't even see the water very well but the rivers are there, and they are important as boundaries, recreation facilities, even sources of energy for power generation. What are their names? Where is their source, and where do they join other rivers or deposit their waters and the soils of upland areas into the sea? How many miles must one drive between San Antonio and Dallas? What highway would one take to make the trip? Your son

wants to attend Abilene Christian University—where is
it? You want to raft on the Attoyac River or fish at Sam
Rayburn Reservoir—where do you go to do so?

Each of us centers a universe from a "home base," or
orientation point, and the rest of the universe is related
to that home base in distances, meanings, and
interlocking relationships in our minds. Justin Wilson
tells a Cajun story about a traveler who asked a small
boy for directions only to find out the youngster could
not provide it. "You don't know nothing," the
frustrated traveler shouted; "No," said the boy, "but I
ain't lost, either."

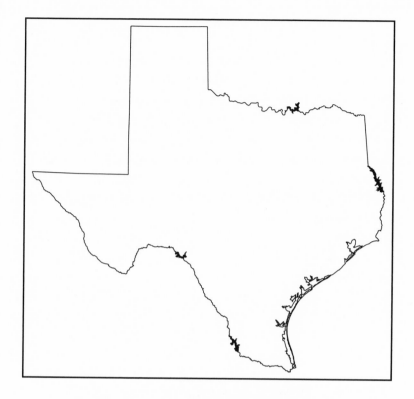

Landmarks

Try locating the following places on the map of Texas by placing the number of the item as close as possible to where it belongs:

1. The State Capital
2. The Big Bend
3. The Alamo
4. Toledo Bend
5. La Reunion Tower
6. Padre Island

7. Spindletop
8. Six Flags Over Texas
9. Johnson Space Center
10. The Tandy Center
11. Chamizal Dispute area
12. San Felipe de Austin

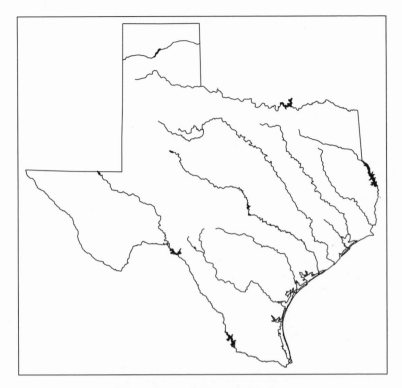

Rivers and Boundaries

Texas is a state with water problems. In the east there is sometimes too much and in the west there is usually never enough. We have prophets who claim that one day water will cost more than oil, and when you look at your water bill during the summer months, you may think this prophesy has already come to pass. Texas does have many rivers and reservoirs; some are for power generation but virtually all of them serve as recreation sites.

On the map, locate the following rivers:

13. Colorado
14. Sabine
15. Nueces
16. Pecos
17. Trinity
18. Red
19. Brazos
20. Neches
21. Guadalupe
22. San Jacinto

Most of the rivers flow northwest to southeast, or they flow into streams that do so. Since the Spaniards tended to cross Texas on a southwest to northeast path, and later arriving Anglo-Americans mostly traveled in the opposite direction, all had to cross many rivers, adding difficulty to the journey, especially before ferries and bridges were established. Another problem was that none of the rivers offered much opportunity for water transportation in Texas, at least not for boats of sufficient size to carry cargo or passengers on a predictable schedule for much distance. Still, rivers are not merely obstacles to transportation. Many of them have served or still serve as political boundaries and are important sources of water for agriculture or recreation, among other uses. Identify the river described:

23. Serves as a boundary between Texas and Louisiana. _____

24. Serves as a boundary between Texas and Oklahoma. _____

25. Serves as a boundary between Texas and Mexico.

26. It is in East Texas and empties into Sabine Lake.

27. It begins in New Mexico, flows through central Texas to the Gulf of Mexico, and is the longest river in Texas. _____

28. It was disputed by Mexico and the U.S. as a boundary in 1846. _____

29. The river associated with Judge Roy Bean. _____

30. Starts in the San Juan Mountains of Colorado but reaches the Gulf of Mexico. _____

31. Flows across the Panhandle from New Mexico to Oklahoma. _____

32. Joins the San Antonio River to flow into San Antonio Bay. _____

Bonus: Give yourself a point if you can answer this question: What water source is associated with Pearl beer?

Lakes, Reservoirs, and "Fishing Holes"

Whether navigable or not, Texas hosts a great volume of flowing water. Much of that water has been impounded into lakes and reservoirs, covering over 400,000 acres. The purpose for such impoundment is usually a combination flood control, power generation, recreation, and urban and industrial requirements. Recreation means such things as boating, water skiing, and diving, of course, but to many it comes down to fishing. Probably every lake in Texas still has the "big one that got away"; the one that grows larger both from the fisherman telling his story and from natural maturity.

If you want to go fishing, where would you find the following lakes and reservoirs? What river was impounded to form these lakes?

33. Amistad _____

34. Choke Canyon _____

35. Lewisville _____

36. Livingston _____

37. Possum Kingdom _____

38. Ray Hubbard _____

39. Sam Rayburn _____
40. Tawakoni _____
41. Texoma _____
42. Toledo Bend _____

Highways

In the nineteenth century, Texans and horses were inseparable. The fabled cowboy never walked when he could ride. Many Texans still fork a horse if they get a chance. But most of us now ride in autos and trucks and regard it as a fundamental right that the road from here to there shall be paved. Clearly, it was not always so. Until 1917, when the first highway department was created in Texas, road work fell to counties or to the individuals who lived along any particular road. Even with a state agency to plan and supervise road construction, Texans remained in the mud and the dust for several more decades. Texas' outstanding farm-to-market road system was not established until 1949, and it was not until the Federal Aid Highway Act of 1956 that the massive ninety-percent-federal to ten-percent-state dollar match gave the state its modern system of highways with over 70,000 miles of paved surface, over 3,000 in divided interstate highways.

Let's see what you know about this road system:

43. The private agency that worked so hard before 1917 to "get Texas out of the mud" was? _____

44. The interstate that approximates the path of U.S. 66 in the Texas Panhandle is? _____

45. The principal Texas city the highway in question 44 serves on an east-west corridor is? _____
46. The first city in Texas reached on I-10 when arriving from Louisiana is? _____
47. Two highways designated as "interstates" are wholly within Texas. What are they? _____
48. The two interstate highways that converge in Reeves County, west of the Pecos, are? _____

---

49. The north-south interstate that divides to offer service to Dallas and Fort Worth is? _____
50. The interstate from Galveston to Dallas is? _____

---

51. The interstate from Texarkana to Dallas is? _____

---

52. The oldest road in the state (not yet an interstate) is? _____

State Capitals

People who deal with state agencies or even state-wide organizations often feel as if those who live and work in our state capital regard it as the center of the universe. It is the nerve center of Texas politics and government (related and intertwined, but not necessarily the same thing), and, with modern transportation, about as centrally located and accessible as any place in Texas. But it was not always so. When President Mirabeau Lamar established the capital in Austin, his political rivals regarded the location as dangerously exposed to raids from hostile Indians or Mexican soldiers.

The location of the capital had changed several times already. Where was the capital located when:

53. Texas was first claimed by Spain? _____
54. Texas became a province under the administration of New Spain? _____
55. The Marquis de Aguayo established his headquarters in Texas in 1720? _____
56. Texas declared independence from Mexico? _____

---

57. Interim President David G. Burnet awaited word of the Alamo? _____
58. Burnet fled to escape Santa Anna's army on its eastward campaign? _____
59. Burnet met with Santa Anna to negotiate an end to war? _____
60. Houston assumed the presidency from Burnet? ____

---

61. Houston moved the capitol to a site offered by J. K. and A. C. Allen? _____
62. Mirabeau Lamar selected a site in 1840? _____

---

63. Houston resumed the presidency in 1841? _____

---

64. Texas became a state? _____

National Forests

Largely due to motion pictures and television, people the world over think all of Texas resembles Leslie Benedict's first view of her new home in the film *Giant*. Not so, East Texans would argue. Not always tropically verdant, at least their part of the state is "green" most of the time. That is the case in Texas' four national forests.

Here are the counties in which these forests are located; supply the name of the forest:

65. Montgomery, Walker, and San Jacinto _____
66. Houston and Trinity _____
67. Angelina, San Jacinto, Jasper, and Nacogdoches __
_____
68. Sabine, Shelby, and San Augustine _____

Cities and Counties

Anglo Texans began county government in 1836 with only twenty-three counties; today there are 254. It is sometimes useful to know the county in which some cities are located.

In the following lists, match each city to the county where it is located. Don't worry if one county is left over—an extra is thrown in for good measure:

69. Georgetown	a. Val Verde
70. Texarkana	b. Ector
71. Lufkin	c. Smith
72. Huntsville	d. Bell
73. Bryan	e. Bowie
74. Port Arthur	f. Brewster
75. Kingsville	g. Houston
76. Laredo	h. Kleberg
77. Del Rio	i. Walker
78. San Angelo	j. Angelina
79. Marathon	k. Jefferson
80. Odessa	l. Nolan
81. Sweetwater	m. Tom Green
82. Tyler	n. Brazos
83. Crockett	o. Webb
84. Temple	p. Duval
	q. Grayson

In this exercise, fill in the name of the county in which the cities in the column are located:

85. Longview _____

86. Beaumont _____

87. Houston _____

88. Austin _____
89. Waco _____
90. Fort Worth _____
91. San Antonio _____
92. Brownsville _____
93. Abilene _____
94. Dallas _____

Colleges and Universities

To what city would you take a young scholar who decided to enroll in one of the following institutions?

95. Sam Houston State University _____
96. Southwest Texas State University _____
97. UTEP _____
98. Texas A&M University _____
99. Austin College _____
100. Southwestern University _____
101. The University of Texas _____
102. Stephen F. Austin State University _____
103. Panola Junior College _____
104. West Texas State University _____
105. Baylor University _____
106. East Texas State University _____
107. Texas Tech University _____
108. Lamar University _____
109. Texas A&I University _____
110. The University of North Texas _____
111. Southern Methodist University _____
112. Rice University _____
113. Prairie View A&M University _____
114. Texas Southern University _____
115. Texas Woman's University _____

116. Tarleton State University _____
117. Texas Christian University _____
118. McMurry College _____
119. Midwestern University _____
120. Pan American University _____
121. Sul Ross University _____
122. Hardin-Simmons University _____

Hurricanes

Texans brag about everything, even weather. We must have the best or the worse; why else would we continue to live where it is either too humid or too arid, so cold at Dalhart or so hot at Marfa or Palacios, or where we are likely to blow away in a tornado. The biggest blows, however, are the tropical storms that kiss our shores and continue across the state leaving debris from high winds and torrential rains. From 1818 to 1885 hurricanes struck at least twenty-five times; sixty-six more times from 1885 to 1964. Since hurricanes have been named for people (first only female names, but now both genders lend names to these mighty forces of nature) only recently, some of these questions will have to be answered with other data.

123. The Texas coastal city and port that was completely washed away by a hurricane in 1886 was? _____

124. The "Great Galveston Storm," the worst natural disaster in U.S. history, occurred in what year? ___

125. In June 1957, Hurricane Audrey struck where? ___

126. In September 1961, Hurricane Carla struck what Texas city? _____

127. In September 1967, Hurricane Beulah devastated Yucatan, then came north to what Texas city with 140 mile-per-hour winds, spawning 115 tornados?

128. Hurricane Celia is known by what distinction among tropical storms in Texas? _____

129. What wind velocity qualifies a tropical storm to be called a hurricane? _____

This-n'-That

Finish this section with questions that deal with a more general knowledge about the natural, political, and cultural geography of Texas.

130. What is the only county in Texas named for a woman? _____

131. What agreement established the Rio Grande as our border with Mexico? _____

132. The Alabama-Coushatta Indian Reservation is located in what county? _____

133. Our state capital, Austin, was located near what pre-existing community? _____

134. The geologic fault zone that curves from Del Rio to the Red River and separates the Edwards Plateau from the coastal plains is known as? _____

135. What is the best known recreational site in central Texas, a.k.a., Austin's "swimming hole?" _____

136. Bastrop was known originally by what name? _____

137. The official flower of Texas is? _____

138. The island where Cabeza de Vaca was shipwrecked was (is)? _____

139. Two narrow, parallel strips of forest running between the 96th and 99th parallels from Oklahoma to central Texas are known as? _____

140. A community near Conroe in Montgomery County received what unique name from a disagreement over a new church steeple? _____

141. In what well-known Lee County city did the National March of Dimes campaign begin in 1944?

142. What style of Texas house involves two structures that share a common roof with an open space between? _____

143. Who was the Spaniard who first mapped the coast of the Gulf of Mexico from Florida to Vera Cruz? __

144. What city in Hardin County is named for a famous spa in New York state? _____

145. Where is the national wildlife refuge for whooping cranes? _____

Answers

1. The State Capital (Austin)
2. The Big Bend
3. The Alamo (San Antonio)
4. Toledo Bend
5. La Reunion Tower (Dallas)
6. Padre Island
7. Spindletop (Beaumont)
8. Six Flags Over Texas (Arlington)
9. Johnson Space Center (near Houston)
10. The Tandy Center (Fort Worth)
11. Chamizal Dispute area (El Paso)
12. San Felipe de Austin

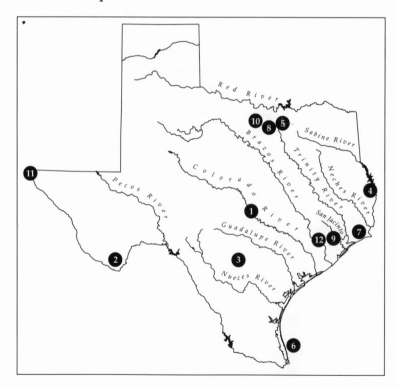

23. Sabine River
24. Red River
25. Rio Grande
26. Neches River; also Sabine River, but you used that answer for #23.
27. Brazos River
28. Nueces River
29. Pecos River
30. Rio Grande
31. Canadian River
32. Guadalupe River

Bonus Answer: "The Land of 1100 Springs," near Leakey, in the area of the Frio River.

33. Amistad is located on the Rio Grande. It covers 64,900 acres and has a storage capacity of 3,497,400 acre-feet.
34. Choke Canyon is located on the Frio River. It covers 26,000 acres and has a storage capacity of 700,000 acre-feet.
35. Lewisville is located on the Elm Fork of the Trinity River. It covers 23,280 acres, and has a storage capacity of 464,500 acre-feet.
36. Livingston is on the Trinity River. It covers 82,600 acres and has a storage capacity of 1,750,000 acre-feet.
37. Possum Kingdom is located on the Brazos River. It covers 17,700 acres and has a storage capacity of 569,380 acre-feet.
38. Ray Hubbard is located on the East Fork of the Trinity River. It covers 22,745 acres and has a storage capacity of 490,000 acre-feet.
39. Sam Rayburn is located on the Neches River. It

covers 114,500 acres and has a storage capacity of 2,876,300 acre-feet.

40. Tawakoni is located on the Sabine River. It covers 36,000 acres and has a storage capacity of 1,135,000 acre-feet.

41. Texoma is located on the Red River. It covers 89,000 acres and has a storage capacity of 2,722,000 acre-feet.

42. Toledo Bend is located on the Sabine River. It covers 181,600 acres and has a storage capacity of 4,472,900 acre-feet.

43. Texas Good Roads Association, founded at a convention in Houston in 1895.

44. I-40.

45. Amarillo.

46. Orange.

47. I-37, Corpus Christi to San Antonio; I-27, Lubbock to Amarillo.

48. I-10 and I-20.

49. I-35 becomes I-35E and I-35W south and north of Dallas-Fort Worth.

50. I-45.

51. I-30.

52. Founded in 1691, the Camino Real was known as the Old San Antonio Road or the King's Highway. In some areas of central and East Texas it approximates the route of State Highway 21. It began at Presidio del Rio Grande and forked into various routes across South Texas to San Antonio, where the roads diverged again, coming together at Nacogdoches before continuing to Louisiana.

53. Mexico City; there was no provincial capital when Spain first claimed the area.

54. Saltillo, 1824–1833; Monclova, 1833–1836.

55. Los Adaes, in northwestern Louisiana near Robeline, where the Marquis de Aguayo headquartered in 1721. It remained the capital for half a century.

56. Washington-on-the-Brazos, the site of the second meeting of the Consultation, where they declared independence on March 2, 1836.

57. Harrisburg, on Buffalo Bayou, where Burnet and his government awaited the outcome of military events in April 1836.

58. Galveston, where Burnet fled to escape Santa Anna's army.

59. Velasco, where Burnet and Santa Anna negotiated the agreement that ended the Texas movement for independence in May 1836.

60. Columbia, later West Columbia, the capital from September to December 1836.

61. Houston, named for the first popularly elected president of the Republic of Texas by its developers.

62. Austin, located near the village of Waterloo, named in honor of Stephen F. Austin, *empresario*, civilian and military leader, and eventually regarded as the Father of Texas.

63. Washington-on-the-Brazos, where Houston determined to serve his second term as president. When he tried to move government records there from Austin in 1842, the consequence was the "Archives War," which resulted in the presidency and the records occupying different capitals.

64. Austin, where James Pinckney Henderson—the first governor of the State of Texas—served, beginning in 1845.

65. Sam Houston National Forest

66. Davy Crockett National Forest
67. Angelina National Forest
68. Sabine National Forest
69. q. Grayson County in central Texas
70. e. Texarkana is in Bowie County—extreme northeastern Texas.
71. j. Lufkin is in Angelina County in the heart of the Piney Woods.
72. i. Huntsville is in Walker County, and hosts, among other things, Sam Houston State University and "The Walls," or the historic state penitentiary.
73. n. Bryan is in Brazos County near Texas A&M University.
74. k. Port Arthur is in Jefferson County in the southeastern corner of Texas.
75. h. Kingsville is in Kleberg County near the headquarters of the fabled King Ranch.
76. o. Laredo is in Webb County across the Rio Grande from Nuevo Laredo.
77. a. Del Rio is in Val Verde County, northwest of Laredo and west of San Antonio.
78. m. San Angelo is in Tom Green County, southwest of Abilene.
79. f. Marathon is in Brewster County and guards the gateway to Big Bend National Park.
80. b. Odessa is in Ector County and is one of the headquarters of the Texas oil industry.
81. l. Sweetwater is in Nolan County, located west of Abilene.
82. c. Tyler is in Smith County in East Texas.
83. g. Crockett is in Houston County, located on the Old San Antonio Road west of Nacogdoches.
84. d. Temple is in Bell County between Austin and Waco.

85. Longview is in Gregg County.
86. Beaumont is in Jefferson County.
87. Houston is in Harris County.
88. Austin is in Travis County.
89. Waco is in McLennan County.
90. Fort Worth is in Tarrant County.
91. San Antonio is in Bexar County.
92. Brownsville is in Cameron County.
93. Abilene is in Taylor County.
94. Dallas is in Dallas County.
95. Huntsville. Founded in 1879 as Sam Houston Normal Institute. State supported.
96. San Marcos. Founded in 1903 as Southwest Texas Normal School. State supported.
97. El Paso. Founded in 1914 as State School of Mines and Metallurgy, later known as College of Mines and Metallurgy and Texas Western College, and now The University of Texas at El Paso. State supported.
98. College Station. Founded in 1876 as the Agricultural & Mechanical College of Texas. A land-grant institution, it is state supported.
99. Sherman. Founded in 1852; originally located in Huntsville. Affiliated with the Presbyterian Church.
100. Georgetown. Founded in 1873 as Texas University. Affiliated with the Methodist Church.
101. Austin. Founded in 1883. Stated supported.
102. Nacogdoches. Founded in 1923 as Stephen F. Austin Teachers College. State supported.
103. Carthage. Founded in 1948. Publicly supported.
104. Canyon. Founded in 1910 as West Texas State Normal College. State supported.
105. Waco. Founded in 1846. Affiliated with the Baptist

Church until 1991; thereafter an independent institution with Baptist heritage.

106. Commerce. Founded in 1917 as East Texas Normal College. State supported.

107. Lubbock. Founded in 1925 as Texas Technological College. State supported.

108. Beaumont. Founded in 1923 as South Park Junior College. Became four-year institution early in the 1950s as Lamar State College of Technology, then Lamar University in 1971. State supported.

109. Kingsville. Founded in 1954 as Texas College of Arts and Industries. State supported.

110. Denton. Founded in 1911 as North Texas Normal College. Also known as North Texas State Normal College, North Texas State Teachers College, North Texas State College (later University). State supported.

111. Dallas. Founded in 1915. Affiliated with the Methodist Church.

112. Houston. Founded in 1912 as The Rice Institute. Private endowment.

113. Prairie View near Hempstead. Began in 1855. Known as Alta Vista Agricultural College, Prairie View State Normal School, Prairie View State Normal & Industrial College, and Prairie View A&M. Land-grant institution with state support.

114. Houston. Founded in 1947 as Texas State University for Negroes. State supported.

115. Denton. Founded in 1902. Also known as Texas State College for Women. Land-grant institution with state support.

116. Stephenville. Founded in 1893. Also known as Stephenville College, The John Tarleton College,

and John Tarleton Agricultural College. State supported.

117. Fort Worth. Founded at Thorp Spring in 1873 as Add-Ran Christian University. Name changed in 1902 and moved to Fort Worth in 1910. Affiliated with Disciples of Christ Church.

118. Abilene. Founded in 1923. Affiliated with the Methodist Church.

119. Wichita Falls. Founded in 1922. Also known as Wichita Falls Junior College and Hardin Junior College. State supported.

120. Edinburg. Founded in 1927. Also known as Edinburg Junior College. State supported.

121. Alpine. Founded in 1920 as Sul Ross State Normal College. State supported.

122. Abilene. Founded in 1891. Also known as Abilene Baptist College and Simmons College (later University). Affiliated with the Baptist Church.

123. Indianola. Formerly known as Powderhorn and later Karlshaven by German immigrants who came through the port to occupy lands in central Texas, the city was devastated by a storm in 1875 and began to dwindle. Its death blow came from another hurricane in 1886.

124. September 8–9, 1900. With winds estimated at 120 miles per hour and a flow of tidal waters covering the island, an estimated 6,000 to 8,000 persons perished and every building was destroyed or damaged.

125. At the Louisiana-Texas border. On June 27, 1957, this storm came inland near the state border with Louisiana, causing extensive damage in Jefferson and Orange counties but even greater damage and

loss of life in Cameron and Calcasieu parishes in Louisiana.

126. Galveston. September 8–14, 1961. Carla was strongest at Galveston and Port Lavaca but was sufficiently large to inflict damage from Port Arthur to Corpus Christi, causing the evacuation of 250,000 persons.

127. Brownsville. September 20–21, 1967. Mostly confined to South Texas, Beulah severely damaged the area's shrimp fleet and did property and crop damage in the amount of $150 million.

128. The most destructive storm in Texas history. August 3, 1970. Celia was "dryer" than most storms, delivering less than torrential rains, but high winds caused losses in excess of $500 million to buildings and $100 million in crops.

129. Seventy-five-mile-per-hour winds qualify a tropical storm to be regarded as a hurricane.

130. Angelina County, located in East Texas, was organized in 1846 and named for an Indian woman.

131. Treaty of Velasco, concluded by Texas' Interim President David G. Burnet and Mexican President Antonio Lopez de Santa Anna on May 14, 1836.

132. Polk County. The Alabama-Coushatta Indian Reservation was created by the state legislature in 1854 and enlarged in 1954.

133. Waterloo, Travis County, settled by Joseph Harrell in 1835. Mirabeau Lamar visited the site in 1837 and decided it was just the spot for a state capital.

134. Balcones Escarpment, a geologic fault zone consisting of several faultings with water-bearing formations.

135. Barton Springs, near the junction of Barton Creek

and the Colorado River, where clear spring water emerges from a fissure.

136. Mina, named for Francisco Xavier Mina, was founded in 1834. Located in Bastrop County on the bank of the Colorado River, the town was incorporated in 1837 and renamed in honor of the Baron de Bastrop.

137. Bluebonnet *(Lupinus texensis)*, adopted by the twenty-seventh legislature as the state flower on March 7, 1901.

138. Galveston Island, also called Mulhado and Isla de Culebras (Island of Snakes). Some Louisiana historians dispute this location, claiming that Cabeza de Vaca landed instead on an island near their state.

139. Cross Timbers, including the Eastern (Lower) Cross Timbers and the Western (Upper) Cross Timbers. Both differ greatly from the prairie features which predominate in the region.

140. Cut 'n Shoot.

141. Dime Box received its unique name from the practice of its postman, John Ratcliff, who did shopping chores for area residents. He placed a box at the store for residents to deposit a ten-cent fee for his services.

142. Dogrun, dogtrot, or breezeway style. Wind drawn through the area provided a cool place that often attracted dogs and humans seeking relief from the hot Texas summer.

143. Alonzo Alvarez de Pineda, commissioned in 1519 to explore the coast of the Gulf of Mexico. He mapped the coastline from Florida to Vera Cruz.

144. Saratoga, located in the Big Thicket, was named for

the famed spa in New York because of seven medicinal springs discovered there by J. F. Cotton.

145. Aransas National Wildlife Refuge, located on a peninsula between San Antonio Bay and Saint Charles Bay, was established in 1937. Administered by the United States Fish and Wildlife Service, it is a haven for several endangered species, including the whooping crane.

3

Why Famous?

Texans and things about their state are famous—and
sometimes infamous or notorious—known across the
United States and abroad. By definition, "fame" carries
a positive connotation; "notorious" will fit here for some
of the other Texans mentioned. One of the most
notorious events in Texas history was the assassination
of John F. Kennedy in November 1963. The tragedy will
always be associated with Texas and is known world
wide as illustrated by an anecdote published in *Reader's
Digest*. The writer described a train ride through Europe
in the 1960s. One compartment included several
travelers who did not share a common language. As
they neared international boundaries, the companions,
divided by their native tongues, helped each other to
complete the various forms required by customs.
Depending on the language of the country

they were entering, the one who spoke that language assisted the others. Our writer was an American and dreaded the moment when the interrogator asked his place of birth. When he said, "Dallas, Texas," the others turned with hands and forefingers extended like a pistol and said, "Bang, Bang." Obviously, they had heard of Dallas and not in a positive way.

There are many positive things about Texas, however, and most of the questions that follow involve them. In the first section, indicate why a person, place or event is famous.

1. Clara Driscoll _____
2. Pompeo Coppini _____
3. Columbus M. "Dad" Joiner _____
4. Andrew Jackson Hamilton _____
5. Julian Onderdonk _____
6. Belle Starr _____
7. James Taylor White _____
8. Cal Farley _____
9. J. Frank Dobie _____
10. Light Crust Doughboys _____
11. Audie Murphy _____
12. Jimmie Rodgers _____
13. Albert Thomas _____
14. Robert E. B. Baylor _____
15. George Catlin _____
16. Norris Wright Cuney _____
17. Pat Garrett _____
18. Estevanico _____
19. Jane Long _____
20. Charles William Post _____
21. St. Denis _____
22. Swen Swenson _____

23. Amon Carter _____

24. Janis Joplin _____

25. Bob Wills _____

26. Angelina _____

27. Matilda Lockhart _____

28. Jared E. Groce _____

29. Henry A. McArdle _____

30. Antonio Margil de Jesus _____

31. Elisabet Ney _____

32. Adolphus Sterne _____

33. Dan Blocker _____

34. Ima Hogg _____

35. Bill Pickett _____

36. Charles Joseph Whitman _____

37. Helena Dill Berryman _____

38. Dick Dowling _____

39. Charles Goodnight _____

40. Anthony Lucas _____

41. Alexander W. Terrell _____

42. Elijah Myers _____

43. Blind Lemon Jefferson _____

44. Tex Ritter _____

45. Adolph Toepperwein _____

46. John Barclay Armstrong _____

47. Martín Perfecto de Cós _____

48. Sieur de La Salle _____

49. Pamela Mann _____

50. Prince Carl _____

51. Zachary Scott _____

52. Isaac L. Ellwood _____

53. Thomas Braniff _____

54. Adina de Zavala _____

55. Anne Sheridan _____

56. James F. Smathers _____

57. Carry Nation _____

58. J. Frank Norris _____

59. Peter Ellis Bean _____

60. Alfred H. Belo _____

61. Gail Borden _____

62. Albert Sidney Burleson _____

63. John Wesley Carhart _____

64. Richard King _____

65. Francis R. Lubbock _____

66. C. W. Macune _____

67. Cynthia Ann Parker _____

68. Mrs. Percy Pennybacker _____

69. Anna Raguet _____

70. Felix Houston Robertson _____

71. Alphonse de Saligny _____

72. Joseph D. Sayers _____

73. Henry Hopkins Sibley _____

74. Ashbel Smith _____

75. Louis T. Wigfall _____

76. John R. Brinkley _____

77. Henry Cohen _____

78. Minnie Fisher Cunningham _____

79. Frank Hamer _____

80. Scott Joplin _____

The next section will deal with things, places, or events.

81. *Lively* _____

82. San Antonio de Valero _____

83. Treaty of 1819 _____

84. Alamo Cenotaph _____

85. Warren Commission _____

86. Lady In Blue _____

87. WBAP-TV _____

88. KUHT-TV _____

Every Texan has to move around to do business in this vast state, and that means one needs to know where the hotels are located. Match these famous hotels with the city in which they are located. Some are no longer in existence.

89. The Menger Hotel
90. The Adolphus Hotel
91. The Driskill Hotel
92. The Edson Hotel
93. The Excelsior Hotel
94. The Nimitz Hotel
95. The Shamrock Hotel

a. Dallas
b. Houston
c. Beaumont
d. Fredericksburg
e. San Antonio
f. Jefferson
g. Austin

For the concluding section of this chapter, identify the famous Texan described:

96. Western gunman killed on July 13, 1881, by Pat Garrett. _____

97. Established a cabin on the east bank of the Trinity River in 1841. _____

98. Author of *Bring 'Em Back Alive.* _____

99. Congressman, famous Tennessee bear hunter, and hero of the Alamo. _____

100. Free black in Nacogdoches who aided Sam Houston in negotiations. _____

101. Union general who proclaimed the Civil War ended in Texas. _____

102. The female slave of Mrs. Jane Wilkinson Long who shared her hardships on Bolivar Peninsula. _____

103. The man accused of assassinating President John F. Kennedy. _____

104. The man who drilled the first oil well in Texas. ___

105. Motion picture actress who starred in the film *Forever Amber*. _____

106. Founder in 1913 of a Dallas school for young ladies. _____

107. Chairman of the Board of the *Houston Chronicle*, secretary of commerce under Franklin Delano Roosevelt, and head of Reconstruction Finance Corporation. _____

108. Country and western singer best known for songs "Four Walls" and "He'll Have To Go." _____

109. First woman state senator in Texas. _____

110. Convicted killer of the accused assassin of President John F. Kennedy. _____

111. Native of Vernon, nationally known jazz trombone player associated with the "big band" era. _____

112. *Ad interim* president of Texas between the closing of the second Consultation and the beginning of the presidency of Sam Houston. _____

113. Conducted major *entrada* across the Southwest, 1540–1542, seeking gold for Spain. _____

114. Plainsman, Indian trader, whose name graces the first cattle trail leading through Indian Territory.

115. Principal writer of the Texas Declaration of Independence. _____

116. Pioneer trail driver and partner of cattleman Charles Goodnight. _____

117. Aviation pioneer killed in a crash in Alaska with humorist Will Rogers. _____

118. According to legend and some Texas historians, the man who refused to cross William B. Travis' line and fled from the Alamo. _____

119. Kiowa chief who led the raid at the Salt Creek Massacre. _____

120. Texas senator who introduced the Eighteenth Amendment to the U.S. Constitution. _____

121. Mexican revolutionary who raided along the Texas border, killed Americans, and eventually was pursued by the American Expeditionary Force commanded by General John J. Pershing. _____

122. Football coach of quarterback Bobby Layne who introduced the "T" formation. _____

123. Commanded the Flying Tigers during World War II. _____

124. Commander of part of the 7th Cavalry who was killed at the Battle of Little Big Horn. _____

125. Railroad entrepreneur who allegedly condemned Jefferson to having grass grow in its streets and bats fly from its belfries because the town would not subsidize his railroad. _____

126. **Bonus:** Take credit if you get this one but don't count it against your score if you don't know it.

In the 1950s, three Texas-born public officials served as president of the United States, U.S. Senate majority leader, and speaker of the U.S. House of Representatives. Who were they?

President _____

Majority Leader _____

Speaker _____

Answers

1. Clara Driscoll is noted for "saving" the Alamo from complete destruction. By the time she became involved with the old church-fortress in 1903, it was in ruins. Driscoll battled private interests and state government successfully, and instilled the care of the Alamo as a sacred trust to the Daughters of the Republic of Texas.
2. Pompeo Coppini sculpted the Cenotaph, or monument, on view in San Antonio's Alamo Plaza since 1939.
3. Joiner discovered the giant East Texas oil field near Kilgore on October 3, 1930, when his Daisy Bradford No. 3 well came in.
4. Andrew Jackson Hamilton was Abraham Lincoln's appointee to start Reconstruction in Texas. After the Civil War he became the first provisional governor of Texas under military occupation and was a leading personality in Texas politics in the 1860s and 1870s.
5. Julian Onderdonk, an artist from San Antonio, specialized in painting scenes of that area.
6. Belle Starr, or Myra Maybelle Shirley, moved with her family to Texas after the Civil War and lived near Dallas; first married Jim Reed and joined him in the outlaw life in the 1870s. After Reed's death she married Sam Starr. She was killed by an assassin.
7. James Taylor White (ca. 1800–1874) is known as Texas' first major Anglo-American cattleman. His JTW brand was the first recorded in Texas.
8. In 1939 Cal Farley, a famed athlete, founded Cal

Farley's Boys Ranch at Old Tascosa (near Amarillo) for youths in need of guidance.

9. J. Frank Dobie (1888–1964) was a noted literary figure who wrote mostly on Texas and southwestern subjects. He taught at the University of Texas and served as editor and secretary for the Texas Folklore Society.

10. The Light Crust Doughboys were a western band who performed for a Fort Worth radio station, beginning in 1931. They became associated with the political campaigns of their sponsor, W. Lee O'Daniel. Original members were Bob Wills, Herman Arnspiger, and Milton Brown.

11. Audie Leon Murphy (1924–1971) from near Farmersville, was the most decorated soldier in World War II. Later he became an actor and appeared in numerous films, mostly westerns, and in the movie version of his autobiography, *To Hell and Back* (1949).

12. James Charles (Jimmie) Rodgers (1897–1933) was born in Meridian, Mississippi, lived his final years in Kerrville, and died of tuberculoses in New York City. A singer of country and folk music, especially about railroads, he was known as "The Singing Brakeman." Among his best known recordings were "The Blue Yodel" and "T For Texas."

13. Albert Thomas (1898–1966) lived in Nacogdoches before moving to Houston. Thomas represented the Eighth District in the U.S. Congress from 1936 until his death in 1966. He played a major role in locating the Johnson Space Center near Houston and entertained President John F. Kennedy at dinner in Houston shortly before Kennedy's

assassination in Dallas on November 22, 1963.

14. Robert Emmett Bledsoe Baylor (1793–1853) organized the Texas Union Baptist Association in 1841, which eventually established a college, now Baylor University.

15. George Catlin (1796–1872), noted painter of Indian life, came to Texas in 1834 with the First Dragoons and lived and painted for a time among the Waco, Comanche, and Tawakoni Indians.

16. Norris Wright Cuney (1846–1897) led the Negro Screwmen's Benevolent Association, the first black labor union in Texas, and also led the Republican Party in Texas in the 1890s.

17. Patrick Floyd (Pat) Garrett (1850–1908) is credited with killing the notorious outlaw William Bonney, better known as Billy The Kid. Garrett lived in Dallas County in 1869.

18. Estevanico, or Stephen the Moor, was among the survivors of a shipwreck in the 1520s on the Texas coast. He was with Alvar Nuñez Cabeza de Vaca and two others when they were rescued. Later he accompanied Fr. Marcos de Niza in an effort to locate Cibola—the legendary cities of gold that Spaniards imagined to be waiting for them in the Southwest.

19. Jane Herbert Wilkinson Long (1798–1880), wife of filibuster Dr. James Long, was among the first known white women of Anglo descent in Texas. She was the mother of one of the first white children born in Texas. After losing her husband, Jane returned to Mississippi, but eventually came back to Texas and is known as "The Mother of Texas."

20. Charles William Post (1854–1914) developed

Postum, Post Toasties, and other food products in Battle Creek, Michigan, before moving to Texas in 1885 to operate ranches in Garza and Lynn counties.

21. Louis Juchereau de St. Denis (1676–1744), an agent of French governor Cadillac, crossed Texas to the Rio Grande in 1714 to establish the presence of his nation. Arrested by Commandant Diego Ramon but treated more like a guest, he returned in 1716 with Domingo Ramon when the Spaniards founded six missions in East Texas and western Louisiana.

22. Swen Magnus Swenson (1816–1896), a Swedish immigrant, lived in LaGrange and Austin until the Civil War and was responsible for bringing many of his countrymen to Texas. With the coming of war, he moved to New York where he became wealthy from Wall Street investments.

23. Amon Giles Carter (1879–1955) was a Fort Worth publisher, businessman, and philanthropist.

24. Janis Joplin (1943–1970) was born in Port Arthur and gained fame as a rock singer during the 1960s. Her gravely voice and involvement in the drug culture made her famous; she died of an overdose of drugs in 1970. Joplin's "Me and Bobby MaGee," one of her most popular recordings, was released posthumously.

25. James Robert (Bob) Wills (1905–1975) was born near Kosse in Limestone County. He played with the Light Crust Doughboys for Governor W. Lee O'Daniel before moving to Tulsa and founding the Texas Playboys. Wills, who played fiddle, is known as the "Father of Western Swing." Among his best-known recordings is "San Antonio Rose."

26. Angelina was a Hainai Indian for whom Angelina

County is named; it is the only county in Texas named for a woman.

27. Matilda Lockhart (ca. 1825–??) was captured by Comanche Indians in 1838 and carried into the Guadalupe Mountains. She was delivered to San Antonio in 1840 with part of her nose burned off and the outrage this produced, plus the failure of the Comanche to deliver other known captives, resulted in the Council House Fight on March 19, 1840.

28. Jared E. Groce (1782–1836) was a member of the Old 300 settlers, Stephen F. Austin's original colony. Said to be the wealthiest man in the colony, Groce also is credited with building the first cotton gin in Texas. Sam Houston's army camped on Groce's Bernardo Plantation during the San Jacinto campaign.

29. Henry Arthur McArdle (1836–1907), born in Ireland, is among Texas' leading nineteenth-century painters. Perhaps his best known works are "Dawn At The Alamo" and "The Battle of San Jacinto," on display in the state capitol.

30. Fr. Antonio Margil de Jesus (1657–1726), guardian of the college of Nuestra Senora de Guadalupe de Zacatecas, accompanied Domingo Ramon to East Texas in 1716 to found the Spanish missions there.

31. Elisabet Ney (1833–1907), sculptor, was born in Europe and became an established artist there before migrating to Texas in 1872 with Dr. Edmund Montgomery. Following Montgomery's death, she returned to sculpting and created statues of Stephen F. Austin and Sam Houston for the Texas exhibit at Chicago's Columbian Exposition in 1893.

Examples of her work may be seen in the state capitol.

32. Nicholas Adolphus Sterne (1801–1852), a native of Germany, migrated to the United States in 1816 and to Nacogdoches in 1826. Sam Houston satisfied Mexican law by accepting Catholic baptism in Sterne's home. Sterne served in the Texas legislature. He left a diary filled with information about life during the period of the Republic.

33. Dan Blocker (1928–1972), born in Bowie County, played "Hoss" on the television series *Bonanza* for thirteen seasons and was co-owner of Bonanza steakhouses. Blocker was a graduate of Sul Ross State University.

34. Ima Hogg (1875–1956), daughter of Governor James Stephen Hogg, became a philanthropist known for the endowment of her home, Bayou Bend, as a museum and a living farm complex at Winedale, among other things.

35. Bill Pickett (ca. 1860s–1932), black cowboy and performer in rodeos and wild-west shows, was best known as a bulldogger.

36. Charles Joseph Whitman (1941–1966), was the infamous "Tower Gunman." On August 1, 1966, Whitman killed members of his family, then killed or wounded several people from the Tower on the University of Texas campus. He was killed by police.

37. Helena Dill Berryman (1804–1888) claimed to be the first Anglo-American born in Texas.

38. Richard W. (Dick) Dowling (1838–1867) commanded Company F, Texas Heavy Artillery, the unit that repulsed General N. P. Banks'

attempted Union invasion at Sabine Pass on September 8, 1863.

39. Charles Goodnight (1836–1929), cattleman, founded the JA ranch in 1877; with Oliver Loving, he established the Goodnight-Loving cattle trail to New Mexico. Goodnight experimented with breeding cattle and buffalo to produce "cattalo." He became a powerful political figure in Texas late in the nineteenth century.

40. Anthony Francis Lucas (Antonio Francisco Luchlich—1855–1921), engineer and oil-well driller, completed the discovery well called the Lucas Gusher in the Spindletop field south of Beaumont on January 10, 1901.

41. Alexander Watkins Terrell (1827–1912) sponsored the Terrell Election Law (1905), which established the primary method of nominating candidates in Texas elections.

42. Elijah E. Myers (1832–1909) designed and supervised the construction of the state capitol building in Austin. It was completed in 1888. He also designed state capitols in Michigan, Colorado, and Utah and the parliament building in Rio de Janeiro.

43. Blind Lemon Jefferson (ca. 1897–1929), born in Wortham, was noted as a composer and performer of blues music.

44. Woodward Maurice (Tex) Ritter (1905–1974), born in Panola County, was a folklorist and graduate of the University of Texas who became an actor and singer in "B" westerns. A member of the Country Music Hall of Fame, Ritter is also remembered for his song "High Noon."

45. In 1906 Adolph Toepperwein (1869–1962), a marksman associated with the Winchester Repeating Arms Company, shot 19,999 out of 20,000 targets—hand-thrown wooden blocks—in a three-day exhibition.

46. John Barclay Armstrong (1850–1913) was the Texas Ranger who captured gunman John Wesley Hardin in April 1877.

47. Martín Perfecto de Cós (1800–1854) commanded the northern provinces under Mexican President Antonio Lopez de Santa Anna. He was defeated at the Battle of San Antonio in December 1835.

48. Rene Robert Cavelier, Sieur de La Salle (1643–1687), established the French presence in Texas in 1685 when his ships arrived at Matagorda Bay. He erected Fort St. Louis nearby. Two years later he was murdered by his men.

49. Pamela (Mrs. Marshall) Mann, her husband, and two sons arrived in Texas in 1834. During the San Jacinto campaign, Sam Houston used her yoke of oxen to pull the "Twin Sisters," two cannon recently arrived from Cincinnati. Mann thought her stock was en route to safety in Nacogdoches. When Houston's army turned south for battle, Mann reclaimed her oxen over Houston's protest.

50. Prince Carl of Solms-Braunfels (ca. 1800–??), a member of the *Adelsverein,* initiated the first German settlements in Texas in the 1840s. New Braunfels is named in honor of the prince's estate on the Lahn River in Germany.

51. Zachary Thomson Scott, Jr. (1914–1965), born in Austin, became a noted stage and motion picture actor. He was nominated for an Academy Award

for his performance in *The Southerner* and is also remembered for his performance in *Mildred Pierce* with Joan Crawford.

52. Isaac L. Ellwood (1833–1910), with partner Joseph F. Glidden, was one of the developers of barbed wire. After 1889 he owned ranches in the Lubbock area.

53. Thomas Elmer Braniff (1883–1954) founded the first passenger air service in the Southwest. It was headquartered at Love Field in Dallas.

54. Adina Emilia de Zavala (1861–1955), descendant of Lorenzo de Zavala, was instrumental in saving the Alamo when she secured a promise from the firm of Hugo and Schmelzer to sell the property to her even before she became a member of the Daughters of the Republic of Texas. Later she vied with Clara Driscoll for control of the property.

55. Anne (Clara Lou) Sheridan (1915–1967) was born in Denton and billed as the "oomph" girl by Paramount Studios after making her film debut in the 1930s. She is best known for the movie *The Man Who Came To Dinner*.

56. James Field Smathers (1888–1967), born on a farm in Llano County, invented the electric typewriter.

57. Carry Amelia (Moore) Nation (1846–1911), prohibitionist, led the crusade against alcohol and tobacco, allegedly using a hatchet to chop up places that sold such sinful items.

58. John Franklyn Norris (1877–1952) was a fiery Baptist preacher. As pastor of Fort Worth's First Baptist Church—by 1925 the largest congregation of that denomination—Norris led a fundamentalist crusade to rid his denomination of liberals in the

1920s and 1930s. He was especially anxious to purge the teaching staff at Baylor University.

59. Peter Ellis Bean (1783–1846), filibuster, was captured with survivors of Philip Nolan's 1801 mustanging expedition into Texas and imprisoned; when released, he returned to the United States but later served in the Mexican army.

60. Alfred H. Belo (1839–1901), publisher of the *Galveston News,* founded the *Dallas Morning News* in 1885.

61. Gail Borden (1801–1874) founded the *Telegraph and Texas Register* at San Felipe on October 10, 1835, and also published at Harrisburg, Columbia, and Houston. He invented the process of preserving condensed milk in a vacuum, or "canning," in 1853.

62. Albert Sidney Burleson (1863–1937) was a congressman and postmaster-general in the administration of President Woodrow Wilson.

63. John Wesley Carhart (1834–1917), San Antonio physician, is credited by the American Manufacturers' Association with inventing the automobile, or "car," while a resident of Racine, Wisconsin, before moving to Texas.

64. Richard King (1825–1885), with partner Mifflin Kenedy, founded the King Ranch in South Texas in 1852 on the Santa Gertrudis grant.

65. Francis Richard Lubbock (1815–1905) was a legislator and Confederate governor of Texas (1861–1863).

66. Charles William Macune (1851–1940), a resident of Burnet, was founder and first president of the National Farmer's Alliance and Cooperative Union of America, organized at a convention in Waco.

The alliance advocated relief for the nation's farmers, particularly in the South.

67. Cynthia Ann Parker (1827–1864), captured by Comanches during a raid in 1836, was raised by Indians and became the wife of Peta Nacona, by whom she had several sons, including noted Comanche chief, Quanah Parker. Returned to her original family in 1860, she never adjusted to the separation from her Comanche family.

68. Mrs. Percy V. (Anna McLaughlin Hardwick) Penneybacker (1861–1938) wrote a standard history of Texas for schools in 1888 that remained a favored text for decades.

69. Anna Raguet (1819–1883) was the romantic interest of Sam Houston early in the 1830s. She later married Dr. Robert Irion, who served as Houston's secretary of state in his second presidential administration.

70. Felix Houston Robertson (1839–1928), grandson of *empresario* Sterling Robertson, became a brigadier-general in the Confederate army in 1864, one of the few Texans to achieve such rank in the Civil War. He was also the last surviving general officer in the Confederate army.

71. Jean Peter Isidore Alphonse Dubois de Saligny came to Texas as an agent of France in 1839 to gather data for his country and to recommend its diplomatic role regarding the Republic. He became involved in the "Pig War" in Austin when his hotel keeper's pigs consumed corn reserved for Saligny's horses, resulting in his filing an unfavorable report about Texas affairs.

72. Joseph Draper Sayers (1841–1929) was the Progressive governor of Texas from 1899 to 1903.

73. General Henry Hopkins Sibley (1816–1886) was a member of the United States army, general in the Confederate army, and served in the Egyptian army following the Civil War. Sibley invented the conical-shaped Sibley tent used for decades by the U.S. Army.

74. Ashbel Smith (1805–1886) was surgeon-general of the Texas army, diplomat, and founder of the University of Texas.

75. Louis Trevesant Wigfall (1816–1874), of Marshall, replaced Sam Houston in the U.S. Senate in 1859 and represented Texas in the Confederate senate.

76. Dr. John Romulus Brinkley (1885–1942) developed the famous "goat-gland transplant" (allegedly a cure for male impotence) and other questionable medical practices. He founded of a powerful 75,000-watt radio station in Villa Acuna, Mexico, near Del Rio.

77. Rabbi Henry Cohen (1863–1952) of Galveston assisted thousands of European Jews through immigration, including finding them homes throughout the central United States.

78. Minnie Fisher Cunningham (1882–1964) led the fight for woman's suffrage in Texas through the Texas Equal Suffrage Association and helped secure ratification of the Nineteenth Amendment.

79. Francis (Frank) Augustus Hamer (1884–1955) was the retired Texas Ranger, called back to service by Governor Miriam Ferguson, who searched for and killed outlaws Clyde Barrow and Bonnie Parker near Gibsland, Louisiana, on May 23, 1934.

80. Scott Joplin (1868–1917), noted black composer and performer of ragtime music, was perhaps best known for "The Entertainer."

81. The thirty-ton schooner *Lively* brought the first settlers to Stephen F. Austin's colony in November 1821.

82. San Antonio de Valero Mission was founded in 1718 by Fr. Antonio de San Buenaventura Olivares of the College of Santa Cruz de Queretaro. The mission chapel is now known as the Alamo.

83. The Treaty of 1819, also known as the Adams-Onis Treaty, provided the first specific boundary between the United States territory purchased from France in 1803 and Spanish territory. The eastern boundary was fixed at the Sabine River north to the 32nd parallel, then north to the Red River and along that stream to the 100th degree, then north to the Arkansas River, then northwest to the Rocky Mountains.

84. The Alamo Cenotaph, created by artist Pompeo Coppini in 1939, is located in Alamo Plaza in San Antonio.

85. The Warren Commission, named for its chairman Chief Justice Earl Warren, was charged with investigating the assassination of President John F. Kennedy in Dallas on November 22, 1963.

86. Maria de Jesus de Agreta, or the Lady in Blue, experienced the Miracle of Transportation while living with a religious order in Spain. While in a trance, she was "transported" to Texas where she converted Indians to Christianity before the arrival of formal missions; mission priests testified to the Indians' familiarity with Christian concepts.

87. WBAP-TV, located in Fort Worth, went on the air on September 27, 1947, and is the oldest television station west of the Mississippi River.

88. Houston's KUHT-TV was founded in 1953 and is

the oldest educational television station in the United States.

89. e. San Antonio
90. a. Dallas
91. g. Austin
92. c. Beaumont
93. f. Jefferson
94. d. Fredericksburg
95. b. Houston
96. William Bonney (1859–1881), also known as Billy the Kid.
97. John Neely Bryan (1810–1877), who is credited with founding the city of Dallas.
98. Frank Buck (1884–1950), famed hunter, author, and motion picture producer, wrote this book in 1931.
99. David (Davy) Crockett (1786–1836).
100. William Goyens (1794–1956), blacksmith and businessman, who came to Nacogdoches in 1820.
101. General Gordon Granger (1822–1876) arrived in Galveston on June 19, 1865, and proclaimed the Civil War ended and war-time measures in effect, including the Emancipation Proclamation.
102. Kiamatia, also called Kiam, continued to serve Jane Long after her relocation to Texas.
103. Lee Harvey Oswald (1939–1963), said by the Warren Commission to have been the single gunman who assassinated the president in Dallas on November 22, 1963.
104. Lyne Taliaferro Barret (1832–1913) began exploring for oil in East Texas late in the 1850s. Following the Civil War he successfully drilled the first oil well in Texas, completing the project in September 1866. It was also the first well located west of the Mississippi River.

105. Linda (Monetta Eloyce) Darnell (1923–1965), from Dallas, became a major motion picture actress before graduating from high school. She starred in *Forever Amber* in 1946, among many others.

106. Ela Hockaday (1875–1956) became headmistress of a young ladies finishing school—equal in quality to eastern establishments—in Dallas.

107. Jesse Holman Jones (1874–1956).

108. James Travis (Jim) Reeves (1923–1964) was one of the early "cross-over" C&W singers. He was also successful in popular music. Reeves died in an airplane crash near Nashville.

109. Margie Elizabeth Neal (1875–1971) served in the Texas senate from 1927 until 1935.

110. Jack Ruby (1911–1967), a Dallas night-club operator, shot Lee Harvey Oswald on Sunday, November 24, 1963, in the parking garage of the Dallas police headquarters as Oswald was being moved to another location. The crime was witnessed live on television by much of the nation.

111. Weldon Leo (Jack) Teagarden (1905–1964); Teagarden also performed as a vocalist with his band.

112. David Gouverneur Burnet (1788–1879) served as interim president of Texas for eight months. He was elected by the Reconstruction government to represent Texas in the U.S. Senate but was not permitted to serve because reconstructed Texas had yet to be recognized by congress.

113. Francisco Vasquez de Coronado (1510–1554), governor of Nueva Galicia, conducted an exploration of the Southwest, including part of Texas, after Alvar Nuñez Cabeza de Vaca told his rescuers of great caches of gold to the north.

Coronado found no gold but did discover Palo Duro Canyon and observed the vast herds of buffalo on the plains.

114. Jesse Chisholm (??–1868), born in Tennessee, moved to Arkansas with the Cherokee migration and lived among and traded with the Indians. The Chisholm Trail bears his name because the first cattle drive north to Kansas in 1866 allegedly followed tracks made a year earlier by his wagons for at least part of the route. There is some disagreement among historians about the validity of this claim.

115. George Campbell Childress (1804–1841), former editor of the *National Banner* and *Nashville Advertiser*, moved to Texas in 1835 after the death of his wife. He was elected to the Consultation from Robertson's Colony only a few weeks after arriving in Texas and was appointed chair of the committee to draft the Declaration of Independence. Childress' proclamation closely follows the form of Thomas Jefferson's declaration of American independence from England.

116. Oliver Loving (1812–1867) was a cattleman who became associated with Charles Goodnight after the Civil War and participated in the drive to Fort Sumner, New Mexico, that began the Goodnight-Loving Trail. Loving was wounded while driving a herd and died in Fort Sumner. Some characters and events of the novel *Lonesome Dove* by Larry McMurtry are based on the association of Goodnight and Loving.

117. Wiley Post (1899–1935), from Grand Saline, piloted the *Winnie Mae* to several aviation achievements but crashed with Will Rogers on board while flying

in Alaska in 1935. Post developed an early version of the pressure suit that has become well known in the age of space exploration.

118. Moses (Louis) Rose (ca. 1785–ca. 1850), from France, came to Texas after serving in Napoleon's army, where he allegedly had enough of war and dying. Rose left the Alamo on March 3, 1836, after accepting the inevitable loss of the fortress. Afterward he made his home in Nacogdoches and later near Logansport, Louisiana.

119. Satanta (ca. 1807–1878), one of the leaders in the Salt Creek Massacre in 1871, was convicted for his crime and sentenced to be hanged; the sentence was commuted, and later he was pardoned by Governor E. J. Davis. When he returned to raiding he was sent to the penitentiary at Huntsville, where he committed suicide by jumping from a window.

120. Morris Sheppard (1875–1941), United States Senator from Texas, introduced the Eighteenth Amendment to the U.S. Constitution prohibiting alcohol.

121. Francisco (Pancho) Villa (1877–1923) lured American forces deep into Mexico in the hope their presence would lead to a war that would overthrow the Mexican government. While tensions between the nations did intensify, war in Europe became a higher U.S. priority in 1917.

122. Johnson Blair Cherry (1901–1966) coached at the University of Texas from 1946 to 1949, won one Southwest Conference championship, and established a record of 32-10-1.

123. Claire Lee Chennault (1890–1958), born in Commerce, commanded the Flying Tigers, or the

American Volunteer Group, in China fighting for Chiang Kai-shek. They became the 14th Air Force in 1943.

124. General George Armstrong Custer (1839–1876) arrived in Texas in 1865 as a part of the Union occupation and headquartered in Austin. He was killed by Sioux Indians at the Battle of the Little Bighorn in Montana on June 25, 1876.

125. Jay Gould (1836–1892), Wall Street operator and developer of the Texas & Pacific Railroad, allegedly made this threat but recent scholarship has discredited the claim.

126. President—Dwight D. Eisenhower; Majority Leader—Lyndon B. Johnson; Speaker—Sam Rayburn.

4

Who Wrote That Book, Song, and so on?

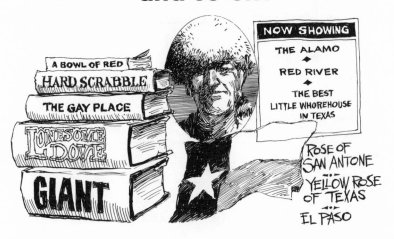

exans indulge themselves in the arts. In literature, some prefer the Bard of Avon and others find J. Frank Dobie, even Louis L'Amour more to their liking. Some folks attend the opera, the ballet, or the symphony, while others prefer George Strait, Clint Black, or Barbara Mandrell.

Texas in Print

This section starts with books. I have borrowed some titles from *The 50 Best Books on Texas* (Dallas: Pressworks Publishing, 1982) by A. C. Greene, then added a few questions of my own about Texas books and authors.

No claim is made that these are the "best" books about Texas, but they are representative.

Identify the author and add a line about content on the following titles. In the answer section, you will find the name of the author, publisher, date of publication, and a comment about the book.

1. *Coronado's Children* _____
2. *Horseman, Pass By* _____
3. *The Great Plains* _____
4. *13 Days To Glory* _____
5. *The Mexican Side of the Texas Revolution* _____
6. *Great River: The Rio Grande in North American History* _____
7. *The Raven* _____
8. *Horse Tradin'* _____
9. *Giant* _____
10. *The Life of Stephen F. Austin, Founder of Texas, 1793-1836* _____
11. *Texas* _____
12. *Lonesome Dove* _____
13. *Not Without Honor: The Life of John H. Reagan* _____

14. *Lone Star: A History of Texas and Texans* _____
15. *The Longhorns* _____
16. *The Texas Rangers: A Century of Frontier Defense* _____

17. *A Texan Looks At Lyndon: A Study In Illegitimate Power* _____
18. *Getting Better All The Time* _____
19. *Papers Concerning Robertson's Colony in Texas* _____

20. *No Name On The Bullet: A Biography of Audie Murphy* _____

Filming Texas

Motion picture technology developed before the end of the nineteenth century, but films did not replace live performances for mass entertainment until the second and third decades of the twentieth century. When "talkies" replaced the "silent" films of the teens and twenties, movies became the primary entertainment medium—and also the primary educational and informational medium.

Many movies have little to offer in the way of entertainment, but all of them teach. I am convinced that most of what the average citizen knows about history comes from movies more than any other source. Things were not always as they are depicted in films—particularly historical portrayals—but unless the history is really bad little harm is done. Many historians are also film buffs, and most do not allow minor inaccuracies to mar a couple hours of entertainment. We even play a trick on ourselves: forever more my mind's eye will see the image of Richard Widmark as James Bowie, even though I know the moon-faced Bowie lacked the Teutonic features of the actor who portrayed him in John Wayne's *Alamo*.

The fact is film makers have not looked at Texas with

indifference. Enough movies about the myth and reality of the Lone Star State have been made that they are the subject of an entire volume—*Cowboys and Cadillacs: How Hollywood Looks at Texas* (Austin: Texas Monthly Press, 1983)—by University of Texas professor Don Graham. Many of the answers to the questions that follow can be found in Graham's book.

After two questions about "Texas" movies in general, the others will concentrate on films made since 1940.

26. How many movies have been made about the Alamo? _____

27. What Texas subject has been the object of the most movies? _____

Texas cities have figured prominently in the movies. The following questions list the principal actors who have appeared in films that include the name of a Texas city in the title; provide the name of the city in question. All these films have been made since 1940.

28. Starring Errol Flynn, Alexis Smith, and S. Z. Sakall, this film deals with Reconstruction difficulties. ____

29. Starring William Holden, MacDonald Carey, William Bendix, and Mona Freeman, this film is the saga of three outlaws who join the Texas Rangers.

30. Gary Cooper, Ruth Roman, Steve Cochran, and Leif Ericson star in another Reconstruction-era film based in a North Texas City. _____

31. Bambi Wood, Richard Boller, Eric Edwards, and Misty Winter starred in a pornographic film about "cheerleading" for a Texas football team. _____

Bonus: Okay. That last one was a disservice to the city and the state. Try this: (1979) Nick Nolte, Mac Davis, Charles Durning starred in another film about the same team.

The following sentences describe a plot; provide the title and the primary star of the film.

32. Tom Dunson, his partner Grout, and young Matthew Garth come to Texas to establish the "first" cattle ranch in South Texas. _____

33. Bio-picture of baseball pitcher who lost his leg in a hunting accident, then made a comeback. _____

34. The last of John Ford's three films about the U.S. cavalry, with his favorite actor starring as Kirby York, a Union officer married to a southern belle. Both protagonists worry about their son. _____

35. Bio-picture of Jim Bowie with much emphasis on the Bowie knife. _____

36. Bio-picture of John Wesley Hardin, with emphasis on his reform following imprisonment. _____

37. Intrigue and scheming by some Texans to remain independent, while agents seek acquisition of Texas by the U.S. _____

38. Fictional story of man who left the Alamo to care for families of those who remained. It includes accusations of cowardice and the hero's demonstration of courage in aiding families in the Runaway Scrape. _____

39. Movie version of successful Walt Disney television programs featuring the life of Tennessee's most famous bear hunter. _____

40. Love story of an oil man and a lady in a Texas oil-boom town; when they separate through misunderstanding, she founds an exclusive women's wear store reminiscent of Neiman-Marcus. There is a reunion of lovers at the end. _____

41. Bio-picture of the Texan who became the most decorated fighting hero of World War II. _____

42. Film version of Edna Ferber's novel about modern Texas; some viewers see the King Ranch portrayed as the Reata in the film. _____

43. John Ford's film about the efforts of a Confederate veteran named Ethan to reclaim his niece who has been captured by a Comanche chief named Scar. _

44. Tragic story set on a pre-Civil War farm; the "hero" is a dog that protects the family while the head of the household is away. _____

45. Story of a sheriff, his jailer, and a drunken deputy who hole up in their jail to prevent a prisoner from being freed by his brother's gang. _____

46. Epic story of the defense of an old church in San Antonio against Santa Anna's army, produced and directed by its star. _____

47. The story of a family divided because of Indian wars and because one family member is a half-breed. Set in the 1870s. _____

48. Twentieth-century story of an East Texas patriarch with a proper but unhappy marriage, one well-balanced but illegitimate son, and another son who matures as a result of events. Patriarch is killed. _____

49. Story of a cattle drive to Texas from a ranch in Mexico operated by a dissolute southerner. Characters include a sheriff and a shady character, the rancher's wife and daughter (who is actually the daughter of the shady character). _____

50. Third film version of a family's annual visit to their state's exposition, this time moved from Iowa to Texas. Love complications involve the children of the family. _____

51. Although most of the action takes place in New Orleans, this film is about a Texas farmer who traveled to Sin City to save his true love. _____

52. Two men, and their women, vie with each other to control gambling in Galveston in 1870s, with an obese and obtuse financier keeping the action going for his own profit. _____

53. Film version of Larry McMurtry's novel, *Horseman, Pass By*, featuring conflict on a modern ranch between a father and his son. Their grandson-nephew is torn by loyalty to each. _____

54. Story of a sophisticated Texan who puts on "good ol' boy" airs when he does business in the Big Apple, and hangers-on who constantly want in on the action. _____

55. Story of a white man who had pigmentation changes to experience what life is like for blacks. __

56. Anti-war movie involving accidental beginning of nuclear conflict in which a Texan rides down the first bomb as if he is hazing a bucking horse. _____

57. Political intrigue focused on Washington, involving a plot to overthrow the government by right-wing military zealots with troops from a secret training base located in Texas. Code word was "ECOMCON." _____

58. Story of a poker game in Laredo with a wife succeeding her stricken husband in the game. _____

59. Set in the 1930s, this is the story of a famous outlaw team of a man and a woman. The pair are killed by a Texas Ranger in Louisiana. _____

60. Fictionalized bio-picture of Texas' famed oil-well fire fighter, Red Adair. _____

61. Story of three astronauts, based at and controlled from Houston, who are stranded in space. _____

62. Based on a novel by James Leo Herlihy, a story of a cowboy who finds a very different life in the big city; partially filmed in Texas. _____

63. A Texas Ranger chases a killer to Indian Territory where the Ranger joins forces with a wily deputy marshal and a spunky girl. _____

64. Spoof of Alamo theme featuring renegade Mexican army commander who "recaptures" the Alamo. __

65. Story of a dying west Texas town that revolves around a pool room and a movie theater that mostly shows *Red River*. _____

66. Story of a fugitive and a girl seeking to escape capture by crossing the international border into Mexico; features fast driving and gunplay in a modern setting. _____

67. Story of the hard life of a rodeo rider in modern Texas. _____

68. Bio-picture of "The Law West Of The Pecos," with a nod to history. _____

69. Story of the assassination of President John F. Kennedy that advances the theory that the deed was done as an inside job involving Texas oil millionaires and government officials. _____

70. Story of a jailbreak in which a girlfriend aids the escapee in breaking out of prison; the chase to catch them is supervised by a wily, sympathetic, but determined lawman. Modern setting. _____

71. Bad, bloody film (that has become a cult classic) in which mayhem is committed using a tool of the forest. _____

72. Escape from a Mexican prison with the aid of a helicopter. Set in West Texas. _____

73. Bio-picture of Woodie Guthrie, partly set in West Texas. _____

74. Based on novel by Dan Jenkins, this is the story of professional football in Texas. _____

75. Bio-picture of a kid from Lubbock who wore horn-rim glasses and made a major impact on rock-and-roll music in the 1950s before his death in an airplane crash. _____

76. Pornographic movie featuring a girl who "works" her way into a "position" with the Dallas Cowboy cheerleaders. References to the organization were blocked by court action. _____

77. Another football film, based on a novel by former player Peter Gent. _____

78. Based on a song popularized by Jerry Lee Lewis, this is the story of a Houston man who is suffering through mid-life crisis with a new Porsche and illicit romances. _____

79. This picture either started or capitalized on the national craze for things Texan, especially longneck beers and mechanical bulls. _____

80. Television series based on Larry McMurtry's novel of two old Texas Rangers who take the first cattle drive to Montana. _____

81. Directed by Oliver Stone, this film advances a conspiracy theory on the assassination of a president. _____

82. Bio-picture based on the life and death of a Mexican border dweller who fought Texas Rangers. _____

83. Story (almost) of the famed Chicken Ranch at LaGrange and its "exposure" at the hands of a Houston television personality; based on musical play co-authored by Larry L. King. _____

84. Story of the modern federal policing agency charged with guarding the international boundary near El Paso against illegal entry. _____

85. Story of modern oil-well wildcatting mixed with romance; producer and star filmed the picture in and near Midland. _____

Texas in Song

The first section that follows deals with some "oldies" gleaned from the *Texas Centennial Songbook* (Sesquicentennial Edition), reprinted in 1985 by the Sesquicentennial Committee of Marfa/Presidio County, Inc., with permission of the Turner Company of Dallas, who produced the 1936 edition. The first line of a song is quoted, except when the first line is the title; in that case, an equally well-known phrase is used. Supply the title.

86. "Oh, give me a home, where the buffalo roam . . ." _____

87. "As I was out walking one morning for pleasure, I spied a cow-puncher all riding alone . . ." _____

88. "With his brogan shoes and ov'r-alls, a tougher looking kid, O you never in your life before had saw." _____

89. ". . . Where coyotes howl over me, In a narrow grave just six by three . . ." _____

90. "Come along, boys, and listen to my tale, I'll tell you of the troubles on . . ." _____

91. "A group of jolly cowboys, Discussing plans at ease, Says one, 'I'll tell you something, boys, If you will listen, please . . .'" _____

92. ". . . I spied a young cowboy wrap'd up in white linen, Wrap'd up in white linen as cold as the clay." _____

93. "God bless you Texas, and keep you brave and strong, That you may grow in pow'r and worth, Thru-out the ages long." _____

94. ". . . I have decked it with roses and spangled with dew. Will you come, will you come . . ." _____

95. ". . . Do not think you can escape them, At night, or early in the morn . . ." _____

96. "I wish I was in de land ob cotton, Old times dar am not forgotten . . ." _____

97. ". . . She's the sweetest rose of color, this soldier

ever knew, her eyes are like the diamonds, they
sparkle like the dew . . ." _____

98. "You've all read the beautiful stories, of countries
far over the sea . . ." _____

Songs from more recent periods. . . .

99. "The stars at night, are big and bright . . ." _____
100. "We dance together, my world's in the skies. It's a
fairy-tale land that's come true . . ." _____
101. "The only two things in life that make it worth
livin', is guitars that tune good and firm-feeling
women . . ." _____
102. "When I die, I may not go to heaven, I don't know
if they let cowboys in . . ." _____
103. "Rain dripping off the brim of my hat, sure is cold
today. Here I am walkin' down Sixty Six, wish she
hadn't done me that way . . ." _____
104. ". . . my legs ain't bowed, and my cheeks ain't
tanned, I'm a cowboy who never saw a cow, Never
roped a steer 'cause I don't know how . . ." _____

---

105. "I still hear your seawinds blowing, I still see her
dark eyes glowing, She was twenty-one, When I
left . . ." _____
106. "I wanna go home with the armadillo, Good
country music from Amarillo and Abilene . . ." ___

---

107. "I've got some fond mem'ries of San Angelo, and
I've seen some beauty queens in El Paso . . ." ____

---

108. "Cowboys ain't easy to love and they're harder to
hold. They'd rather give you a song than diamonds
or gold . . ." _____

109. "God painted bluebonnets in the field by a tough little scrub-oak on an east Texas hill . . ." _____

110. "My Ma was born in Dallas, Father in Fort Worth. You can bet your boots I got my roots, In the good old Texas Earth. . . ." (second verse) _____

Answers

1. *Coronado's Children,* by J. Frank Dobie (Dallas: Southwest Press, 1930). A. C. Greene calls this "the book that made it possible for a Texas writer to stay home and make a living" (*The 50 Best Books on Texas,* p. 9).
2. *Horseman, Pass By,* by Larry McMurtry (New York: Harper & Brothers, 1961); *Hud,* starring Paul Newman, is the movie version of the story.
3. *The Great Plains,* by Walter Prescott Webb (Boston: Ginn, 1931); interpretive history of life on the Plains.
4. *13 Days To Glory,* by Lon Tinkle (New York: McGraw-Hill, 1958); the story of the Battle of the Alamo.
5. *The Mexican Side of the Texas Revolution,* by Carlos E. Casteñeda (Dallas: P. L. Turner, 1920); the other point of view.
6. *Great River: The Rio Grande In North American History,* by Paul Horgan (New York: Rhinehart & Co., 1954); history of this great river.
7. *The Raven,* by Marquis James (Indianapolis: Bobbs-Merrill, 1929); biography of Sam Houston.
8. *Horse Tradin',* by Ben K. Green (New York: Alfred A. Knopf, 1967); the wisdom of a lifetime from a veterinarian-writer.
9. *Giant,* by Edna Ferber (Garden City and New York: Doubleday, 1952); story of a family on a large South Texas ranch that many thought represented the King Ranch.
10. *The Life of Stephen F. Austin, Founder of Texas, 1793–1836,* by Eugene C. Barker (paperback edition, Austin: University of Texas Press, 1969); biography of the Father of Texas.

11. *Texas,* by James A. Michener (New York: Random House, 1985); fictional saga of the state's history written for the Sesquicentennial.

12. *Lonesome Dove,* by Larry McMurtry (New York: Simon & Schuster, 1985); story of two old Texas Rangers and their outlaw friend who took the first cattle drive to Montana. It was written with stars John Wayne, James Stewart, and Henry Fonda in mind, but played as a CBS television mini-series with Tommy Lee Jones, Robert Duvall, and Robert Urich.

13. *Not Without Honor: The Life of John H. Reagan,* by Ben H. Procter (Austin: University of Texas Press, 1962); biography of Texas' representative to the Confederate cabinet and first chairman of the Texas Railroad Commission.

14. *Lone Star: A History of Texas and Texans,* by T. R. Fehrenbach (New York: MacMillan, 1968); history of Texas, written with "felicity of style."

15. *The Longhorns,* by J. Frank Dobie (reprint edition, Austin: University of Texas Press, 1980); stories about Texas' legendary livestock.

16. *The Texas Rangers: A Century of Frontier Defense,* by Walter P. Webb (Austin: University of Texas Press, 1980); the history and legends of the Texas law enforcement agency, narrated with admiration for its accomplishments.

17. *A Texan Looks At Lyndon: A Study In Illegitimate Power,* by J. Evetts Haley (Canyon: Palo Duro Press, 1964). In the vain hope that it would bring about LBJ's defeat in his run for the presidency in 1964, this politically biased account was published in the midst of the campaign.

18. *Getting Better All The Time,* by Liz Carpenter (New

York: Simon & Schuster, 1987); about her life as LBJ family confidant and about the author's retirement following a career as a Washington correspondent.

19. *Papers Concerning Robertson's Colony in Texas,* compiled and edited by Malcolm D. McLean (Arlington: University of Texas at Arlington, 1974 through 1993); exhaustive presentation to advance claims to Robertson's role in the founding of Texas.

20. *No Name On The Bullet: A Biography of Audie Murphy,* by Don Graham (New York: Viking, 1989); biography of Texan Audie Murphy, the most decorated serviceman in World War II.

21. *Eats: A Folk History of Texas Foods,* by Ernestine Sewell Linck and Joyce Gibson Roach (Fort Worth: TCU Press, 1989); smorgasbord of Texas foods—how to find, prepare, and enjoy them.

22. *Lone Star Rising: Lyndon Johnson And His Times,* by Robert Dallek (New York: Oxford University Press, 1991); biography of LBJ—more sympathetic than Robert Caro's work.

23. *Duel Of Eagles: The Mexican and U.S. Fight For the Alamo,* by Jeff Long (New York: William Morrow, 1990); highly critical analysis of all things Texan in the movement for independence from Mexico.

24. *The Cowgirls,* by Joyce Gibson Roach (revised and updated edition, Denton: University of North Texas Press, 1990); cowgirls chronicled through every phase of "cowboying" activity.

25. *Helpful Hints for HouseHusbands of Uppity Women,* by Archie P. McDonald (Dallas: E-Heart Press, 1988); this is a "ringer," I'll admit, but I wish every Texan had bought one!

26. The answer has to be subjective. Judging from a list of titles that contain the term "Alamo" or

others that are about the Alamo but do not have that term in the title, the correct answer is ten or eleven at least. They include: *The Immortal Alamo* (1911); *The Martyrs Of The Alamo* (1913); *Davy Crockett At The Fall Of The Alamo* (1926); *West Of The Alamo* (1946); *The Iron Mistress* (1955); *The Alamo* according to Duke Wayne (1960); *The Road To The Alamo* filmed in Italy (1966); *Viva Max!* (1969); *An Alamo Scrapbook* filmed in England (1974); and I remember a Glenn Ford movie called *Man From The Alamo* (1953).

27. The Texas Rangers. Just judging from titles, I count forty-nine. Of those, the Lone Ranger figures in more movies than any other character.
28. *San Antonio* (1945)
29. *Streets of Laredo* (1949)
30. *Dallas* (1950)
31. *Debbie Does Dallas* (1978) Bonus Answer. *North Dallas Forty*
32. *Red River*, starring John Wayne, Walter Brennan, and Montgomery Clift.
33. *The Stratton Story*, starring James Stewart, June Allyson, Frank Morgan.
34. *Rio Grande*, starring John Wayne, Maureen O'Hara, Victor MacLaglen.
35. *The Iron Mistress*, starring Alan Ladd, Virginia Mayo, Phyllis Kirk.
36. *The Lawless Breed*, starring Rock Hudson, Julia Adams, John McIntire.
37. *Lone Star*, starring Clark Gable, Ava Gardner, Lionel Barrymore (as Andrew Jackson), Broderick Crawford.
38. *The Man From The Alamo*, starring Glenn Ford, Julia Adams, Victor Jory, Chill Wills.

39. *Davy Crockett, King Of The Wild Frontier*, starring Fess Parker, Buddy Ebsen.
40. *Lucy Gallant*, starring Jane Wyman, Charlton Heston, Thelma Ritter, Claire Trevor.
41. *To Hell And Back*, based on the life of—and starring—Audie Murphy, Marshall Thompson, Charles Drake.
42. *Giant*, starring Rock Hudson, Elizabeth Taylor, James Dean.
43. *The Searchers*, starring John Wayne, Jeffrey Hunter, Vera Miles, Ward Bond; although filmed in Monument Valley, the story is located in West Texas.
44. *Old Yeller*, based on Fred Gipson's novel, starring Fess Parker, Dorothy McGuire, Tommy Kirk.
45. *Rio Bravo*, starring John Wayne, Dean Martin, Walter Brennan, Angie Dickinson.
46. *The Alamo*, starring John Wayne, Richard Widmark, Laurence Harvey.
47. *Flaming Star*, starring Elvis Presley, Barbara Eden, Dolores Del Rio, John McIntire.
48. *Home From The Hill*, starring Robert Mitchum, Eleanor Parker, George Peppard, George Hamilton, and based on a novel by William Humphrey.
49. *The Last Sunset*, starring Kirk Douglas, Rock Hudson, Dorothy Malone, Joseph Cotton.
50. *State Fair*, filmed at the state fair grounds in Dallas, and starring Pat Boone, Bobby Darin, Ann-Margaret, Pamela Tiffin, Tom Ewell.
51. *Walk On The Wild Side*, starring Laurence Harvey, Jane Fonda, Barbara Stanwyck, Capucine.
52. *Four for Texas*, starring Frank Sinatra, Dean Martin, Anita Ekberg, Ursula Andress.

53. *Hud*, starring Paul Newman, Melvyn Douglas, Patricia Neal, Brandon De Wilde.

54. *The Wheeler Dealers*, starring James Garner, Lee Remick, Phil Harris, Chill Wills.

55. *Black Like Me*, starring James Whitmore, Roscoe Lee Browne, Al Freeman, Jr., Will Geer.

56. *Dr. Strangelove*, starring Peter Sellers, George C. Scott, Sterling Hayden, Slim Pickens.

57. *Seven Days In May*, starring Burt Lancaster, Kirk Douglas, Frederic March, Ava Gardner.

58. *A Big Hand For The Little Lady*, starring Henry Fonda, Joanne Woodward, Jason Robards, Jr., Charles Bickford.

59. *Bonnie And Clyde*, starring Warren Beatty, Faye Dunaway, Michael J. Pollard, Gene Hackman.

60. *Hellfighters*, starring John Wayne, Katherine Ross, Jim Hutton, Vera Miles, Jay C. Flippen.

61. *Marooned*, starring Gregory Peck, Richard Crenna, David Janssen, James Franciscus, Gene Hackman.

62. *Midnight Cowboy*, starring Dustin Hoffman, Jon Voight, Sylvia Miles, John McGiver.

63. *True Grit*, starring John Wayne, Glen Campbell (as the Texas Ranger), Kim Darby, Robert Duvall.

64. *Viva Max!*, starring Peter Ustinov, Pamela Tiffin, Jonathan Winters, John Astin.

65. *The Last Picture Show*, starring Timothy Bottoms, Jeff Bridges, Cloris Leachman, Ben Johnson.

66. *The Getaway*, starring Steve McQueen, Ali McGraw, Ben Johnson, Sally Struthers.

67. *J. W. Coop*, starring Cliff Robertson, Geraldine Page, Christina Ferrare, R. C. Armstrong.

68. *The Life and Times of Judge Roy Bean*, starring Paul

Newman, Jacqueline Bisset, Ava Gardner, Stacy Keach.

69. *Executive Action*, starring Burt Lancaster, Robert Ryan, Will Geer, John Anderson.
70. *The Sugarland Express*, starring Goldie Hawn, Ben Johnson, Michael Sacks, William Atherton.
71. *The Texas Chainsaw Massacre*, starring Marilyn Burns, Allen Danzier, Edwin Neal, Gunnar Hansen.
72. *Breakout*, starring Charles Bronson, Robert Duvall, Jill Ireland, John Huston.
73. *Bound For Glory*, starring David Carradine, Ronny Cox, Melinda Dillon, Gail Strickland.
74. *Semi-Tough*, starring Burt Reynolds, Jill Clayburgh, Kris Kristofferson, Robert Preston.
75. *The Buddy Holly Story*, starring Gary Busey, Don Stroud, Charles Martin Smith, Bill Jordan.
76. *Debbie Does Dallas*, starring Bambi Wood, Richard Boller, Eric Edwards, Misty Winter.
77. *North Dallas Forty*, starring Nick Nolte, Mac Davis, Charles Durning, Dayle Haddon.
78. *Middle Age Crazy*, starring Bruce Dern, Ann-Margaret.
79. *Urban Cowboy*, starring John Travolta, Debra Winger, Scott Glenn.
80. *Lonesome Dove*, starring Tommy Lee Jones, Robert Duvall, Robert Ulrich.
81. *JFK*, starring Kevin Costner, Tommy Lee Jones.
82. *The Ballad of Gregorio Cortez*, starring Edward James Olmos, Barry Corbin.
83. *The Best Little Whorehouse In Texas*, starring Burt Reynolds, Dolly Parton, Charles Durning.
84. *The Border*, starring Jack Nicholson, Valerie Perrine, Warren Oates.

85. *Waltz Across Texas*, starring Terry Jastro, Anne Archer, Mary Kay Place, Noah Berry.
86. "Home On The Range," Traditional.
87. "Whoopie Ti Yi Yo, Git Along Little Dogies," Traditional.
88. "Little Joe, The Wrangler," Traditional.
89. "O Bury Me Not On The Lone Prairie," Traditional
90. "The Old Chisholm Trail," Traditional.
91. "When The Work's All Done This Fall," Traditional.
92. "The Cowboy's Lament," or "The Streets of Laredo," Traditional.
93. "Texas, Our Texas," W. J. Marsh (the official state song adopted in 1929).
94. "Will You Come To The Bower?" Thomas Moore (Irish Folk Tune); played by Sam Houston's "musical corps" of fife and drum at the Battle of San Jacinto.
95. "The Eyes of Texas," Traditional (official song of The University of Texas).
96. "Dixie," Daniel Emmett.
97. "The Yellow Rose of Texas," Anonymous.
98. "Beautiful Texas," W. Lee O'Daniel.
99. "Deep In The Heart Of Texas," June Hershey, Don Swander.
100. "Waltz Across Texas," Talmadge Tubb.
101. "Luckenbach, Texas," Bobby Emmons and Chips Moman.
102. "Texas (When I Die)," Ed Bruce, Bobby Borches, and Patsy Bruce.
103. "Is Anybody Goin' To San Antone," Dave Kirby and Glenn Martin.
104. "I'm An Old Cowhand (From The Rio Grande)," Johnny Mercer.

105. "Galveston," Jimmy Webb.
106. "London Homesick Blues," Gary P. Nunn.
107. "Texas Women," Hank Williams, Jr.
108. "Mamas, Don't Let Your Babies Grow Up To Be Cowboys," Ed Bruce and Patsy Bruce.
109. "No Place But Texas," Alex Harvey (written for the Sesquicentennial celebration).
110. "Giant (This Then Is Texas)," Paul Francis Webster, Dimitri Tiomkin (written for the movie).

5

He (She) Was

Elected to What?

For some Texans, politics are life's breath; for others, they are at least as interesting as sports and not a little unlike gambling. But for all, whether acknowledged or not, politics are important.

During the first seven decades of electing officials, Texans operated on a politics-of-personality system. They voted for "the man," the only gender "available" then, rather than for a party, although some charismatic leaders did establish a kind of a "party" concept, meaning that their supporters generally rallied behind the same issues as did the candidates. Presidents Sam Houston and Mirabeau Lamar, each representing a radically different vision for the Republic of Texas, rallied supporters of like mind; but always it was Houston and Lamar, not the issues, that bound voters.

The only change in this system from the Civil War until the end of the nineteenth century was that political success in Texas required one to be some kind of Democrat; still, within that framework, "personality" determined election. The Progressive Era, roughly 1890 to 1915, witnessed a weakening of the system, or, some might think, a confirmation of it.

Modern, two-party politics did not get cranked up in Texas until early in the 1950s. Despite the state's breaking solidarity with the Solid South by voting for Republican Herbert Hoover in 1928, and the rebellion of the Texas Regulars against the Roosevelt administration early in the 1940s, most Texans could not bring themselves to embrace Republicanism officially, although a great many of them really were Republicans in attitude. After the 1950s, however, party affiliation produced straight-ticket voters in more than one party. It would be inaccurate, though, to say that Texans have shed their affection for individual political figures. We still love our political barbecues and rallies and we like to shake the hands of those for whom we intend to vote—this time. Our loyalties may not be as firm to candidates as in the past, except in special cases (Ann Richards for the Democrats and Phil Gramm for the Republicans, for example), but we yet respond to the Texan tradition of voting for "the man," even if that is as likely now to be the "woman."

The Revolutionary Period

What follows are some tough questions about the early years.

1. The legislation by the Mexican congress that closed off American immigration was? _____
2. The Spanish term for the type of leadership represented by Santa Anna is? _____
3. Who presided at the Convention of 1832 when Texans first expressed a desire to be a separate state of the Mexican Republic? _____
4. The Mexican Republic, under the Constitution of 1824, provided what type of government? _____

---

5. The first attempt at independent government in Texas, though it lasted only eighteen days, was known as? _____
6. Who did the Consultation name as provisional governor of Texas at its meeting in the fall of 1835? _____
7. Who did the Consultation name as interim president when it declared independence at its meeting in the spring of 1836? _____
8. What is Texas Independence Day? _____
9. Who is credited with writing the Texas Declaration of Independence? _____
10. The treaty by which Santa Anna recognized Texas independence was? _____

The Republic

This section ought to be a little easier because it involves some of Texas' best known leaders.

11. Which president of the U.S. has been accused of plotting the Texas Revolution to gain control of the area? _____
12. Who was the first popularly elected president of the Republic of Texas? _____

13. Why was he not elected to a second term when his first term ended? _____

14. Who was the second president of the Texas Republic? _____

15. Which president of the Republic is mostly responsible for the boldness associated with Texas?

16. Who is known by the title, "Father of Texas Education"? _____

17. Who is known as "The Architect of Annexation"?

18. Who said, "The Republic of Texas is no more"? __

19. The personal argument between an Austin hotel keeper and the French minister to Texas is known by what name? _____

20. The "war" that erupted in East Texas in the 1840s over an election dispute is known by what name?

Statehood, Confederacy, and Statehood Again

21. The law that reduced Texas' borders to their present location was embodied in a major legislative package known as? _____

22. During the 1850s Texas received a significant immigration from what European country? _____

23. Who were the first two Texans sent to the U.S. Senate? _____

24. Who received the most votes by Texans for the American presidency in 1860? _____

25. Of the principal candidates for president in 1860,

who received the least amount of votes in
Texas? _____

26. Who presided at the Texas secession convention?

27. At that convention, who said, "Mr. Speaker, when
the rabble hiss, well may patriots tremble" when
others showed disapproval of his vote against
secession? _____

28. Who was governor of Texas when the state voted
for secession? _____

29. When the elected governor refused to swear
allegiance to the Confederacy, who completed his
term? _____

30. Who was the first elected governor of Confederate
Texas? _____

31. Who replaced the first Confederate governor
following elections in 1863? _____

32. Who was appointed by President Abraham Lincoln
as provisional governor to begin Reconstruction in
Texas? _____

33. Who was elected governor of Texas under the
Johnson Plan of Reconstruction? _____

34. When congress rejected the Johnson Plan
governments, who was appointed governor of
Texas by military authority? _____

35. Who was the Radical Reconstruction governor of
Texas? _____

36. What was his legislative program called by most
Texans? _____

37. Notice was served that Texans were tired of Radical
rule at what gathering in Austin in 1871? _____

38. Who defeated the Radical governor in the election
of 1873? _____

39. Those who wanted to regain control of Texas politics from the Radicals were known as? _____

40. This Radical governor sought to retain his office by having the election of 1873 declared illegal. The Texas court that agreed with him became known as? _____

41. The federal agency that helped former slaves adjust to freedom was? _____

42. The post-war governor of Texas who is known for keeping state spending down the best was? _____

43. The governor mentioned above reduced expenditures and raised taxes, including a tax on liquor-by-the-drink. What was that tax called? ____

44. His tax that attempted to gain revenue from companies doing business in Texas but not headquartered in the state—companies that sent out traveling salesmen, for instance—was known as? _____

45. Resentment of railroad and banking practices led Texas farmers to enter politics in the 1870s. The organization that first provided their forum was known as? _____

46. The hottest political issue in Texas from the 1870s until after 1900 was? _____

47. Who was the Progressive attorney general and later governor who attempted to regulate the insurance industry and the railroads? _____

48. What political dispute did he help Governor L. S. Ross settle in Fort Bend County? _____

49. This Progressive governor's wing of the Democratic

Party was known in 1892 by what name? _____

50. The Republican Party was led in the 1890s by what remarkable black leader? _____

Early Twentieth Century Politics

51. Although he never held elective office, the person who dominated Texas politics at the turn of the century was? _____

52. The senator who ran as the "Last Democrat" was?

53. The Progressive Era (1890s–1915) witnessed much change in Texas politics, including what new method of voter registration? _____

54. This voter registration method had to be completed by what date each year to be able to vote in November elections? _____

55. The Progressive Era also ushered in a new method by which political parties nominated candidates. It was called? _____

56. A terrible storm in Galveston in 1900 brought about what innovation in municipal government? _____

57. In 1913, the city of Amarillo introduced what form of municipal government? _____

58. Who was the Texas banker who won rural votes by adopting the nickname of "Farmer?" _____

59. The promise of what legislation won him the most votes? _____

60. This governor is known for what distinction among the state's chief executives? _____

61. What did he call the legislature that provided him with this distinction? _____

62. Senator Joseph W. Bailey of Texas sponsored the Seventeenth Amendment to the U.S. Constitution. It deals with what? _____

63. Senator Morris Sheppard of Texas sponsored the Eighteenth Amendment to the U.S. Constitution. It deals with what? _____

64. Hiram W. Evans of Dallas is known for leading what organization with much political power in the 1920s? _____

65. Evans' group claimed to have elected what U.S. senator from Texas? _____

66. Who was the first woman elected governor of Texas? _____

67. What was her campaign slogan? _____

68. The Democratic Party held its national convention in Houston in 1928 and nominated whom for president? _____

69. W. Lee O'Daniel won the governor's race in 1938. By then, what nickname had this flour salesman, business executive earned from appearing on a daily radio show? _____

70. What country music organization performed on his show and was active in his political campaign?

World War II and After

Most of the rest of this chapter will be more "current events" than "history." What do you know about politics in the 1940s, 1950s, and 1960s?

71. Who served as governor of Texas during World War II? _____

72. Who won and who lost the special senate race in 1941? _____

73. A group of Texas Democrats began to oppose President Franklin D. Roosevelt early in the 1940s. They were known as? _____

74. In 1946, six candidates sought the office of governor. For a while it looked like it was five against one because of a controversy at the University of Texas. Who was at the center of that controversy? _____

75. One candidate held back, claiming to be the only one who could enter the governor's mansion without "mud on my hands." Who was this candidate? _____

76. In 1948, Texas experienced perhaps its most famous political election, a race for the U.S. Senate. Who won and who lost? _____

77. What nickname did the victor earn from this election? _____

78. The election hinged on what precinct in what county? _____

79. The most significant scandal in state politics in the first decade after World War II involved what? ____

80. Other than this scandal, what was the most significant political issue in Texas late in the 1940s and early in the 1950s? _____

81. The governor who led Texans to support the Republican candidate for president in 1952 because of this issue was? _____

82. Texans who followed their governor in this effort became known as? _____

83. What Republican candidate was the first native Texan to become president of the United States? __

84. Who was the Texan who yearned so to be

governor that he gave up a seat in the U.S. Senate for the job in 1956? _____

85. The Texan who ran for president in 1960 but accepted the vice presidency instead was? _____

86. His campaign slogan, used before his defeat at the Democratic Convention, was? _____

87. The Texas governor who had served as Secretary of the Navy in the administration of John F. Kennedy was? _____

88. Kennedy was assassinated in what Texas city? ____

89. The Texas governor who had been a theater operator before serving in public office was? _____

90. He left office after being tainted by, but not indicted in, what major political scandal? _____

Modern Texas Politics

We have reached modern Texas politics—the 1970s to the present. One would expect to do best on this portion of the exercise, but how quickly some things are forgotten.

91. What was the title of the group of House members who opposed Speaker Gus Mutscher in 1971? ____

92. What woman representative emerged from that group and nearly won the Democratic nomination for governor in 1972? _____

93. Who defeated her for the nomination and introduced the slogan "No New Taxes" to politics? _____

94. Name the first Republican from Texas to serve in the U.S. Senate since Reconstruction. _____

95. Name the first Republican governor of Texas since Reconstruction. _____

96. Name the federal judge from Tyler whose decisions have done much to change Texas' legislative and administrative procedures. _____

97. Name the former agriculture commissioner who angered Republicans more than anyone else. _____

98. Name the Treasurer who won the governorship in the state's most expensive campaign. _____

99. Name the candidates she defeated for her party's nomination. _____

100. Name the Republican candidate she defeated. _____

How about a **bonus?** Do you know:

a. The "adopted hometown" of President George Bush?
b. The Texan who served as secretary of state in the Bush administration?
c. The Texan who ran for vice-president in 1988?
d. The presidential candidate with whom he ran?

A Little of This 'n A Little of That

Finish off this exercise on politics with a little "this n' that" which cuts across time. What was:

101. The Capitol Boycott? _____
102. The Capitol Syndicate? _____
103. The Chicken-Salad Case? _____

104. The Gilmer-Aiken Law? _____
105. Greenback Party of Texas? _____
106. Guerrero Decree? _____
107. Hogg Laws? _____
108. Homestead Law? _____
109. Loyal Union League? _____
110. The People's Party? _____
111. Turtle Bayou Resolutions? _____
112. American G.I. Forum of Texas? _____
113. Raza Unida Party? _____

Who was

114. Thomas Terry Connally? _____
115. Martin Dies? _____
116. John Nance Garner? _____
117. Oveta Culp Hobby? _____
118. George Parr? _____
119. Samuel Taliaferro Rayburn? _____

Chief Executives of Texas

Name all the governors of Texas in order. It won't be easy, so the dates of service and other hints are added.

120. Feb. 1845–Dec. 1847 (left office to lead troops in the Mexican War) _____
121. May 1846–Nov. 1946 (filled in while old what's his name went to war) _____
122. Dec. 1847–Dec. 1849 (one of our truly unforgettable leaders) _____
123. Dec. 1849–Nov. 1853 (the first two-term governor)

124. Nov. 1853–Dec. 1853 (shortest tenure) _____

125. Dec. 1853–Dec. 1857 (rivers and railroads) _____

126. Dec. 1857–Dec. 1859 (beat the Hero of San Jacinto)

127. Dec. 1859–Mar. 1861 (would not swear allegiance to the Confederacy) _____

128. Mar. 1861–Nov. 1861 (served until first Confederate governor elected) _____

129. Nov. 1861–Nov. 1863 (first Confederate governor)

130. Nov. 1863–June 1865 (served until the Civil War ended) _____

131. July, 1865–Aug. 1866 (provisional governor to begin Reconstruction) _____

132. Aug. 1866–Aug. 1867 (governor under the Johnson Plan of Reconstruction) _____

133. Aug. 1867–Sept. 1869 (appointed governor by the military commander) _____

134. Jan. 1870–Jan. 1874 (first Republican governor) ____

135. Jan. 1874–Dec. 1876 (Redeemer governor) _____

136. Dec. 1876–Jan. 1879 (took over when previous governor went to senate) _____

137. Jan. 1879–Jan. 1883 (secessionist, jurist) _____

138. Jan. 1883–Jan. 1887 (slowed predecessor's alienation of public land) _____

139. Jan. 1887–Jan. 1891 (Confederate general, later president of Texas A&M University) _____

140. Jan. 1891–Jan. 1895 (created the Railroad Commission) _____

141. Jan. 1895–Jan. 1899 (governor because E. M. House decreed it) _____

142. Jan. 1899–Jan. 1903 (appointed first city commission in Galveston) _____

143. Jan. 1903–Jan. 1907 (saw Terrell Election Law passed) _____

144. Jan. 1907–Jan. 1911 (Progressive governor) _____

145. Jan. 1911–Jan. 1915 (last Progressive governor sponsored by E. M. House) _____

146. Jan. 1915–Aug. 1917 (impeached and removed) ___

147. Aug. 1917–Jan. 1921 (newspaper man) _____

148. Jan. 1921–Jan. 1925 (also president of Baylor University) _____

149. Jan. 1925–Jan. 1927 (first woman governor) _____

150. Jan. 1927–Jan. 1931 (cleaned up pardons scandal)

151. Jan. 1931–Jan. 1933 (cotton acreage control to combat the Depression) _____

152. Jan. 1933–Jan. 1935 (that woman again) _____

153. Jan. 1935–Jan. 1939 (organized the DPS) _____

154. Jan. 1939–Aug. 1941 ("Pass the Biscuits") _____

155. Aug. 1941–Jan. 1947 (conservative, patriotic, and a budget balancer) _____

156. Jan. 1947–July 1949 (solid, compromise candidate, who died on a trip back to Austin) _____

157. July 1949–Jan. 1957 (led Texas to support Republican presidential candidate) _____

158. Jan. 1957–Jan. 1963 (tidelands, and creator of state archives) _____

159. Jan. 1963–Jan. 1969 (Kennedy's secretary of the Department of Navy) _____

160. Jan. 1969–Jan. 1973 (Sharpstown and the movies)

161. Jan. 1973–Jan. 1979 (called the "disappearing governor" because of absences from Austin) _____

162. Jan. 1979–Jan. 1983 (first Republican governor since Reconstruction) _____

163. Jan. 1983–Jan.1987 (attorney general from Houston) _____

164. Jan. 1987–Jan. 1991 (he got even for losing in 1982)

165. Jan. 1991–to present (placed a "silver foot" in someone's mouth) _____

Answers

1. Law of April 6, 1830
2. *caudillo*
3. Stephen F. Austin
4. federal
5. The Permanent Council
6. Henry Smith
7. David G. Burnet
8. March 2
9. George Childress
10. Treaty of Velasco, signed May 14, 1836, at Velasco, by Santa Anna and President Burnet. The treaty also identified the Rio Grande as a boundary for the first time.
11. Andrew Jackson
12. Sam Houston, former governor of Tennessee and commander of Texas forces during the Revolution.
13. The Texas constitution did not permit successive terms of office for the executive branch.
14. Mirabeau Buonaparte Lamar, formerly of Georgia.
15. Lamar. Despite frequent illnesses and being a smaller man than Houston, Lamar advocated independence and expansion while Houston favored joining the United States to solve Texas' problems.
16. Lamar. He was a champion of education, especially for the establishment of a state university.
17. President Anson Jones, elected in 1844. He awarded the title to himself after annexation was achieved during his term of office.
18. President Anson Jones on December 29, 1845, when the Lone Star flag was replaced by Old Glory during ceremonies in Austin.

19. The Pig War. The argument grew from the hotel keepers' pigs raiding corn stored for the minister's horses and ended with the minister, the Comte de Saligny, leaving Texas.
20. Regulator-Moderator War.
21. The Compromise of 1850.
22. Germany; really, several Germanic countries. They mostly arrived on the coast at Indianola and moved inland to settle in Central Texas.
23. Sam Houston and Thomas Jefferson Rusk. Texas' senators are still said to serve in either the Houston or Rusk "succession."
24. Former Vice President John C. Breckinridge of Kentucky, the so-called Deep South candidate.
25. Abraham Lincoln, whose name did not appear on the Texas ballot. Breckinridge polled 47,548 votes; John Bell received 15,465 votes; and Stephen A. Douglas received 410 votes.
26. Oran M. Roberts.
27. James Throckmorton.
28. Sam Houston.
29. Lieutenant Governor Edward Clark.
30. Francis R. Lubbock.
31. Pendleton Murrah.
32. Andrew Jackson Hamilton.
33. James Throckmorton.
34. E. M. Pease, who previously had served as governor from 1853 to 1857.
35. Edmund J. Davis
36. The Obnoxious Acts, which included authority for Davis to appoint a state militia and state police agency, allowed the governor to fill all government vacancies by appointment, and to select an "official" newspaper.

37. The Taxpayers Convention.
38. Richard Coke.
39. Redeemers.
40. The Semi-Colon Court, because they held the election to be illegal on the basis of punctuation in the constitution. Coke was inaugurated anyway, and Davis accepted the verdict of the people.
41. The Freedman's Bureau.
42. Oran M. Roberts.
43. The Bell Punch Tax, so called because the collector punched a hole in a tally sheet, and in the process the punch rang a bell. Ease of cheating and humor caused repeal of the tax.
44. The Drummer Tax, which was declared unconstitutional.
45. Grangers, or officially, the Patrons of Husbandry.
46. Prohibition.
47. James Stephen Hogg.
48. The Jaybird (Democrats)-Woodpecker (Republicans) War.
49. Car Barn Democrats, because they met for their convention in Houston's street car depot, the only facility in town large enough for their meeting.
50. Norris Wright Cuney led "Regular" Republicans; others were known as "Lily-White" Republicans.
51. Between 1890 and 1915, Edward M. House "made" governors, supporting J. S. Hogg, Charles Culberson, Joseph D. Sayers, S. W. T. Lanham, T. M. Campbell, and Oscar B. Colquitt.
52. Joseph Weldon Bailey. He meant that as the last "Bourbon Democrat," and he was not in tune with the Progressive Era.
53. The Poll Tax.
54. By January 31 of each year.

55. The party primary election.
56. The city commission form of government.
57. The city manager form of government.
58. James E. Ferguson.
59. The Farmer Tenant Law, which attempted to establish legal limits on rent shares for sharecroppers.
60. Ferguson is the only governor to be impeached and removed from office. The legislature charged Ferguson with various crimes and misdemeanors ranging from bribery to misappropriation of state funds, but the real reason they wanted him out of office was political.
61. A Kangaroo Court.
62. The election of United States senators by popular ballot rather than by the legislature.
63. The prohibition of the manufacture and sale of alcoholic beverages.
64. The Ku Klux Klan.
65. Senator Earl Mayfield.
66. Mrs. Miriam Amanda ("Ma"—from her initials) Ferguson ran because her husband could not. Soon he became known as "Pa."
67. "Two governors for the price of one."
68. Governor Al Smith of New York.
69. Pappy, from a song, "Pass The Biscuits, Pappy"; the theme song of his radio show.
70. The Light Crust Doughboys; for a time, noted country-swing musician Bob Wills played with the group.
71. Governor Coke Stevenson.
72. Governor W. Lee O'Daniel defeated Congressman Lyndon Baines Johnson by less than 5,000 votes.
73. Texas Regulars.

74. The University of Texas President Homer Price Rainey, who was fired, then ran for governor.
75. Buford Jester.
76. Congressman Lyndon B. Johnson defeated former Governor Coke Stevenson by eighty-seven votes.
77. "Landslide Lyndon."
78. Box 13 in Jim Wells County.
79. The Texas Veteran's Land Board. Some of its members were accused of profiting from funds set aside to assist World War II Texas veterans.
80. Control of the tidelands, or mineral production on the continental shelf of the Gulf of Mexico.
81. Governor Allan Shivers.
82. Shivercrats.
83. Dwight David Eisenhower.
84. Price Daniel.
85. Lyndon Baines Johnson.
86. "All The Way With LBJ."
87. John Bowden Connally.
88. Dallas, on November 22, 1963.
89. Preston Smith.
90. The Sharpstown Scandal, which involved passing legislation to benefit a Houston businessman in return for financial gain.
91. The Dirty Thirty, which included liberals and conservatives who opposed Mutscher's leadership.
92. Frances "Sissy" Farenthold.
93. Dolph Briscoe.
94. John Tower.
95. William P. (Bill) Clements.
96. Judge William Wayne Justice.
97. Jim Hightower.
98. Ann Richards.

99. Former Governor Mark White and Attorney General Jim Mattox.
100. Clayton Williams.

Bonus Answers:

a. While residing in a rather famous public-housing unit in Washington, D.C., Bush claimed a rented hotel room in Houston as his address for voter registration purposes.
b. James Baker of Houston.
c. Senator Lloyd Bentsen.
d. Massachusetts Governor Michael Dukakis.

101. Union action protesting the use of convict labor on the Capitol building project in the 1880s. Result: imported stonemasons from Aberdeen, Scotland.
102. Chicago businessmen who financed the state capitol, then accepted three million acres of state land as payment on which they established the XIT Ranch.
103. One of the charges against Governor James E. Ferguson during his impeachment proceedings was that he had used state money for his own groceries. Ferguson had signed legislation to cover such expenses for his predecessor, Oscar B. Colquitt, including a bill for "chicken salad and punch."
104. Passed in 1949 and named for Senator A. M. Aiken and Representative Claude H. Gilmer, this law established the Teacher Education Agency and set standards and funding formulas for public education in Texas.
105. The Greenback party was founded in Texas in 1874

and ceased to exist in 1884. It advocated the broader use of currency.

106. Decree of Mexican President Vicente Guerrero in 1829 that abolished slavery in Mexico and Texas.

107. Legislation passed during the administration of Governor James S. Hogg included establishing the Railroad Commission, the Stock and Bond Law, and the Alien Land Law, among other laws intended to regulate business for the benefit of Texas patrons.

108. A homestead law has existed in Texas since Spanish days; such laws protect homes and tools of trade from foreclosure.

109. A Republican political organization during the Reconstruction Era to recruit black voters for that party.

110. Popular name for the Populist political organization, first seen in Texas in 1886 when farmers in Comanche County ran a "Farmer's Democratic" slate for local offices. The party claimed 100,000 members, and won 160,000 votes for its gubernatorial candidate, Thomas L. Nugent, in 1894, and 238,000 votes for Jerome Kearby in 1896. The party ceased to exist after 1908.

111. A statement of cause adopted on June 13, 1832, by men who had gathered at Turtle Bayou near Anáhuac to protest the arrest of Americans by the Mexican military. The incident is part of the story of the Texas Revolution.

112. Organized on March 16, 1948, with Hector Garcia as its first chairman, the Forum is involved in civil rights activities, especially for Mexican-Americans.

113. *Raza Unida* (united race or united people), was organized in January 1970 under the leadership of José Angel Gutierrez of Crystal City.
114. U.S. Senator Tom Connally (1877–1963) served as chairman of the Foreign Relations Committee and sponsored the resolution for the U.S. to join the United Nations.
115. Dies (1901–1972) was chairman of the House Un-American Activities Committee which sought to ferret out Nazi and later Communist infiltrators.
116. Garner (1868–1967) served as Speaker of the U.S. House of Representatives from 1931 to 1933 and Vice President from 1933 to 1941.
117. Hobby, the wife of Governor William Pettus Hobby and the mother of Lieutenant Governor William P. Hobby, commanded the WACs during World War II and served as secretary of the Department of Health, Education, and Welfare during the Eisenhower Administration.
118. Parr (1901–1975), also known as the Duke of Duval, is alleged to have delivered the necessary votes that insured the election of Lyndon B. Johnson to the U.S. Senate in the disputed 1948 primary race.
119. Rayburn (1882–1961), known as "Mr. Sam" and "Mr. Speaker," served as Speaker of the U.S. House of Representatives (1940–1947, 1949–1953, and 1955–1961).
120. James Pinckney Henderson
121. A. C. Horton
122. George T. Wood
123. Peter Hansborough Bell
124. J. W. Henderson
125. Elisha M. Pease
126. Hardin R. Runnels

127. Sam Houston
128. Edward Clark
129. Francis R. Lubbock
130. Pendleton Murrah
131. Andrew Jackson Hamilton
132. James W. Throckmorton
133. Elisha M. Pease
134. Edmund J. Davis
135. Richard Coke
136. Richard B. Hubbard
137. Oran M. Roberts
138. John Ireland
139. Lawrence Sullivan Ross
140. James Stephen Hogg
141. Charles A. Culberson
142. Joseph D. Sayers
143. S. W. T. Lanham
144. Thomas Mitchell Campbell
145. Oscar Branch Colquitt
146. James E. Ferguson
147. William P. Hobby
148. Pat M. Neff
149. Miriam A. Ferguson
150. Dan Moody
151. Ross S. Sterling
152. Miriam A. Ferguson
153. James V. Allred
154. W. Lee O'Daniel
155. Coke R. Stevenson
156. Buford H. Jester
157. Allan Shivers
158. Price Daniel
159. John Bowden Connally
160. Preston Smith

161. Dolph Briscoe
162. William P. (Bill) Clements
163. Mark White
164. William P. (Bill) Clements
165. Ann Richards

6

What War Was That?

Texans are militant folk. The Republic of Texas was born of battle, and success in that endeavor led inevitably to a war between the United States and Mexico in which Texans took a zealous and noticeable part. Though most of the participants of these wars had only recently become Texans, the intensity they brought to battle established a tradition of readiness to fight for home and country that has lasted until the modern period. In the American Civil War, the Spanish-American War, World Wars I and II, Korea, and Vietnam, Texans served with distinction, often in high command, and in percentages of population greater than other states.

The first military expeditions in Texas were carried out by Spain's conquistadores, the Spaniards coming in conquest a mere 500 or so years ago. The Spaniards were prepared. Their arsenal included fire arms, horses, trained dogs, armor, and above all a belief in the appropriateness of Spanish dominance. And so they came, and conquered, and when their *entradas* found no gold in Texas—as they had in Mexico and elsewhere to the south—they lingered and were willing to fight to hold on to empty space, if for no other reason than to keep others from obtaining it.

Others also came: First the French, represented by La Salle and St. Denis. Most of all in the twilight of Spanish control came the Americans. The filibusters—Philip Nolan, Augustus Magee, James Long—created the most excitement, but the real work of Americanizing Texas came from that numberless and nameless (except to themselves) majority who filtered in while no one watched the expansive and largely unguarded frontier. They claimed a piece of dirt, erected a dwelling on it, maybe plowed it or just hunted on and near it, and remained ready to defend it always.

Most settlers arriving in Mexican Texas during the 1820s came as "legal" immigrants. They accepted Mexican citizenship and dug in for a long stay. Within a decade, others joined them from the United States for various reasons—more land, adventure, whatever. Together, these pioneers won independence through military action, and established the Republic. Even then they fought Mexican raiders, Indians—especially the Comanche—and sometimes themselves. When their Republic merged with the United States, *los diablos Tejanos* fought in the war with Mexico with a zeal that produced both awe and embarrassment among their non-Texan commanders.

Hood's Brigade, Terry's Texas Rangers, and a host of others carried the Lone Star on their flags and in their hearts to Civil War battlefields in Pennsylvania, Maryland, Tennessee, Mississippi, and Virginia. Then came more Indian wars and a war with Spain, when Rough Riders recruited in Texas joined other Americans to fight (and die mostly of disease) on the islands that represented Spain's last grip on the New World.

There were the world wars, the First—strictly European, except upon the seas, and the Second—virtually everywhere on earth. Texans, again, commanded, fought and endured. And so on through Korea, Vietnam, Grenada, and in Desert Storm in 1991.

Warring and soldiering remain significant in Texas culture. It is time to see what you know about war in and by Texans.

Spain and Mexico

This section begins before anyone in Spain knew anything about "Tejas" and concludes before the start of the Texas Revolution.

1. Those who seized New World land for Spain by force are known by what name? _____

2. Name the Spaniard who led the conquest of Aztecs in Mexico for his nation and for personal benefit.

_____

3. Who was the political and military leader who led an *entrada* across Texas in 1540 seeking cities of gold? _____

4. Spanish activity in the Southwest resulted in the transfer of the horse to Native Americans. Which group of them then developed into the world's best cavalrymen? _____

5. When the Frenchman La Salle arrived in Texas in

the 1680s, what defensive military installation did he build? _____

6. What became of La Salle? _____

7. When the Spaniards established their religious missions in Texas most were accompanied by a garrison of soldiers for protection. This garrison was known by what title? _____

8. When the Spaniards adopted a new policy toward Texas in 1772, who received the duty of making war on the Apache and the Comanche? _____

9. In the 1790s Spanish commanders transferred troops from the Pueblo de San Carlos del Alamo de Parras to San Antonio. The troops occupied the site of what mission and thus attached their name to the site? _____

10. The adventurers who invaded Spanish Texas from the 1790s until 1820 for private gain—but whose activities also advanced the American frontier—are known by what title? _____

11. Who was the person of this type who entered Texas several times claiming that he only wanted to capture mustangs? _____

12. Although this leader was killed, some of his men were captured and sentenced to die for violating Spanish law. Only one of them was executed. Who was he? _____

13. What American commander on the southwestern frontier in the first decade of the nineteenth century was accused of being a double agent for Spain? _____

14. What commander dispatched soldiers to explore the Arkansas River country in 1807. _____

15. What is the name of the "no-man's-land"

established along the Sabine River in 1806 in a agreement between Spanish and American commanders? _____

16. The unruly population which came to live in that unpoliced area were chased out temporarily by what American military officer? _____

17. This officer became unhappy with his lack of advancement in the service, so he joined with what Spanish Republican to declare Texas free from Spain in 1812? _____

18. Although eventually led by others, the movement expired when their soldiers were defeated by troops in a battle near the Medina River in 1813. Who led the victors? _____

19. Who led the band of pirates that occupied Galveston Island early in the nineteenth century?

20. Who led the final major invasion of Spanish Texas in 1819 and 1820 after the U.S. had renounced all claims to land west of the Sabine River? _____

The Texas Revolution and the Republic

The era of the Texas Revolution is the most studied period of our state's history and in some ways the least understood. Mostly we reflect on the glory of San Jacinto and the agony of the Alamo and Goliad, and we see the fight in ethnic terms—Mexican against American. But in the beginning the revolution represented a division of states' rights versus centralist views of government and constitution.

Americans could be found on both sides of the argument, but most settlers who had arrived prior to

1830 remained loyal Mexican citizens even after the first armed clashes in 1832. Gradually they lost faith in the Mexican political system, and when they were joined by increasing numbers of new arrivals from the United States, the scales tipped in favor of those who preferred independence to redress under the Mexican system.

21. Who alarmed Mexican officials during the 1820s by proclaiming his Fredonia Republic independent of Mexico? _____

22. Who was the military commander of the Northern Provinces (including Texas) in 1830? _____

23. Who commanded the Mexican troops stationed at Anáhuac, where the first "Disturbance of 1832" occurred? _____

24. Who commanded Mexican troops in Nacogdoches in 1832? _____

25. How did this commander cause a further "Disturbance of 1832" in Nacogdoches? _____

26. What did John Austin attempt to get past the Mexican military at Velasco that caused the third "Disturbance of 1832"? _____

27. What statement of purpose was adopted by those who gathered to free the prisoners at Anáhuac? ___

28. Who came to Texas under the direction of Santa Anna to investigate the meaning of the "Disturbances of 1832"? _____

29. Who reestablished a Mexican military presence in Texas in April 1835 by order of his brother-in-law, President Santa Anna of the new central republic?

30. Who led the raid on Anáhuac in July 1835 to expel

the Mexican garrison commanded there by Captain Antonio Tenorio? _____

31. Where did the action occur that is said to be "The Lexington of the Texas Revolution"? _____

32. What was lettered on the flag flown by the Texans at that battle? _____

33. When more men gathered at this battle site, who did they elect to be their commander for an assault on San Antonio? _____

34. Who led the assault on San Antonio on December 5, 1835? _____

35. Who led the majority of the victors of the Battle of San Antonio on the ill-fated Matamoros expedition? _____

36. Who commanded in San Antonio after the departure of most of the troops for Matamoros? ___

37. Who commanded several hundred men, mostly new arrivals from the U.S., at Goliad? _____

38. Who came to San Antonio in January 1836 to assist the commander there, then became the commander himself? _____

39. Who commanded the "volunteers" at the defense of the Alamo? _____

40. What engineer prepared the defenses of the Alamo? _____

41. What was the song allegedly played by Santa Anna's musicians at the final assault on the Alamo? _____

42. How many men defended the Alamo? _____

43. Name the man who chose not to remain and defend the Alamo. _____

44. Name the famous American frontiersman from Tennessee who died at the Alamo. _____

45. Who received command of Texas forces from the revolutionary government known as the Consultation? _____

46. Who showed up at Gonzales with fifty riflemen from Kentucky and found himself in command of a regiment? _____

47. Who served as the scout of the Texas forces during the San Jacinto campaign? _____

48. Besides the Alamo, what additional loss did the Texans suffer in March 1836? _____

49. When Texas civilians learned of these losses, their panicked flight was called what? _____

50. What encouraging support did the Texans receive as a gift from the city of Cincinnati while Houston led his army in apparent retreat? _____

51. Under what flag did the Texans fight at San Jacinto? _____

52. What song was played by Texas musicians while marching to battle at San Jacinto? _____

53. Who commanded federal troops along the Sabine River to ensure that Santa Anna would not invade the United States? _____

54. What agreement ended the Texas Revolution as far as the Texans were concerned? _____

55. What name was earned by Isaac Burton's cavalry during the Revolution? _____

56. Who commanded the Texas Navy during the Revolution and for part of the period of the Republic? _____

57. A soldier in the Texas army received how much land from a grateful government? _____

58. During the period of the Republic, President Houston wanted Albert Sidney Johnston to command the army. But Johnston was wounded in

a duel, preventing him from assuming command. Who was the would-be assassin? _____

59. What was Houston's solution to the tension created by the outcome of the duel, and his fear that the army would reopen war with Mexico? _____

60. President Lamar sent a military expedition to what New Mexico town to compel its residents to accept Texas citizenship? _____

Statehood, Civil War, Reconstruction, and the Indian Wars

Over the ten years that Texas remained an independent Republic, some citizens worked to join the United States. They finally achieved their goal on December 29, 1845. This brought renewed war with Mexico. While doubtless more Texans fought in the Mexican-American War than did the citizens of any other state, the vast resources of the United States made the outcome inevitable.

Peace never seemed to last. Within fifteen years seventy-five percent of voting Texans opted to leave the United States and join the Confederacy, which resulted in four more years of war and an even longer time under military rule during Reconstruction. Then came the final showdown with the Indians, especially the Comanche.

61. Who was the U.S. general in command at the Nueces River line when the clashes that produced war with Mexico occurred? _____

62. Name the U.S. general who mounted the nation's first amphibious landing at Vera Cruz from bases in Texas. _____

63. What name was earned by Texans fighting in this war? _____

64. Who was the commander of U.S. forces in Texas when secession occurred? _____

65. Confederate Governor Francis Lubbock called for companies to be organized as the Texas Brigade. By what name did this unit become better known? __

66. What was the best known unit from Texas that fought in the Western Theater of the Civil War? __

67. A number of Texans reached the rank of Confederate general during the Civil War. Who among them, however, was the only native-born Texan? _____

68. Who was the first military commander in Texas for the Confederacy? _____

69. Who was the second and last military commander in Texas for the Confederacy? _____

70. By what nickname was Confederate (and Texas Ranger) commander John S. Ford known? _____

71. Texas was part of the Trans-Mississippi Department. Who was the commander? _____

72. Who was the Texan who claimed the Department of Arizona for the Confederacy? _____

73. Who commanded the Confederate invasion of New Mexico in 1862 and was defeated at the Battle of Glorieta? _____

74. What was the favorite song of most Confederate soldiers from Texas? _____

75. When the Confederates reclaimed control of

Galveston Island in 1862, the soldiers assaulted the island on flat-bottomed boats called what? _____

---

76. Where did artillerymen under Dick Dowling stop a Federal invasion on the Texas coast in September 1863? _____

77. In 1864, General Richard Taylor's forces blocked a second invasion attempt of Texas in what battle? __

---

78. The Civil War ended in Texas by the proclamation of what U.S. army officer? _____

---

79. What was the last battle of the Civil War fought in Texas? _____

80. When occupation troops arrived in Texas, who commanded them? _____

81. What officer among those in the occupation forces later won great fame fighting the Sioux Indians? __

---

82. Under the Reconstruction Acts of 1867, Texas was placed in what military district? _____

83. Who was the first military commander of this district? _____

84. During the Civil War, Texans had to assume their own Indian defense. Who organized the Frontier Regiment for this assignment? _____

85. What famous battle was fought against Indians in the Texas Panhandle during the war? _____

---

86. After the war, many Texas forts were garrisoned by black troops. By what name did these troops come to be known? _____

87. What was President U. S. Grant's post-war Indian policy called? _____

88. What Indian raid helped convince U.S. military leaders that a more active policy was required? ___

89. What Indian leader was convicted and imprisoned for leading this raid? _____

90. Who commanded the great roundup of the Plains Indians in 1874 and marched them to reservations in Indian Territory? _____

World Wars

By the 1890s Texans and many Americans continued to dream of conquest—even though the halcyon times of the frontier years were over. As the country entered the new century, the fighting would go on but the conquering would be outside North America. Already Alaska had been purchased; acquisition of Hawaii would follow. After war with Spain, the Spanish possessions of Puerto Rico, the Philippines, and other islands, as well as special "interests" in Central and South America and in the Orient would fall into American hands. Some of these interests and acquisitions involved military intervention and led the nation—and with it Texas—into world wars with origins in the 1890s.

91. Probably the best-known military unit involved in the Spanish-American war was organized in San Antonio. What was the name of this unit? _____

92. From 1900 until 1917, Texans were more concerned with Mexican revolutionaries than European foes. Who raided into Texas and New Mexico in an effort to provoke the U.S. into eliminating the Mexican president? _____

93. To whom did President Woodrow Wilson assign the task of leading a force against this Mexican leader? _____

94. What diplomatic blunder angered Texans against Germany even before the U.S. declared war on that nation? _____

95. What Texan was President Wilson's personal representative to European governments? _____

96. What Texan chaired the important House Ways and Means Committee during World War I? _____

97. Name the Texan who served on the House Foreign Relations Committee during World War I? _____

98. What notable legislation did Sam Rayburn sponsor during World War I? _____

99. Who established San Antonio as the center for military aviation training in the U.S.? _____

100. Approximately how many Texans served in the armed forces during World War I? _____

101. What Texan introduced the war resolution against Japan in 1941? _____

102. San Antonio served as headquarters for what U.S. Army unit during World War II? _____

103. What Texas training facility was known as "The West Point of the Air"? _____

104. Approximately how many Texans served in the armed forces during World War II? _____

105. How many Texans received the Congressional Medal of Honor? _____

106. Name the Texan who was the most decorated service person of World War II? _____

107. What Texan was the most decorated member of the U.S. Navy during World War II? _____
108. What Texan was the first black hero of World War II? _____
109. How many Texans became general officers during World War II? _____
110. Name the highest ranking army officer who was born in Texas? _____
111. How many Texans became admirals in the U.S Navy during World War II? _____
112. Name the highest ranking naval officer who was born in Texas? _____
113. What Texas woman achieved the highest military rank during World War II? _____
114. How many prisoner-of-war camps were located in Texas during World War II? _____
115. What is the most famous unit that hailed from Texas during World War II? _____

Match these World War II era military installations with their location. An extra site is thrown in just to make it interesting.

116. Fort Bliss	a. Wichita Falls
117. Fort Clark	b. Houston
118. Camp Hood	c. Galveston
119. Fort Sam Houston	d. El Paso
120. Camp Fannin	e. Cuero
121. Camp Mabry	f. Tyler
122. Red River Ordnance Depot	g. Killeen
	h. Austin
123. Fort Travis	i. Texarkana
124. Sheppard Field	j. San Antonio
125. Ellington Field	k. Brackettvile

A Little of This 'n A Little of That

The conclusion of this exercise on military affairs includes a few random questions.

126. What flag flew over the Alamo while Texans defended it? _____

127. What issue was involved in the Archives War? ____

128. Who won and who lost the Battle of Agua Dulce Creek? _____

129. At one time, the Texas revolutionary forces "suffered" from having four commanders-in-chief; who were they? _____

130. Who might be called the "Courier of the Alamo"?

131. Who won and who lost the Battle of Coleto? _____

132. What was the Cordova Rebellion all about? _____

133. The Council House Fight involved what forces; what caused the incident? _____

134. Who were the Davis Guards? _____

135. What was the Grass Fight? _____

136. Who served as Texas' secretary of war and later commanded Confederate forces in the Western Theater during the Civil War? _____

137. What proved to be the decisive battle of the Texas Revolution? _____

138. Who commanded the Second Cavalry Regiment at San Antonio in 1860? _____

139. Who won and who lost the Battle of the Neches?

140. Who recruited the New Orleans Grays for service during the Texas Revolution? _____

141. Who won and who lost the Battle of Palo Alto? ___

142. Name the Confederate brigadier who later served as president of Texas A&M. _____

143. What was the Salt War about? _____

144. What was the Sutton-Taylor Feud? _____

145. What famous battleship is moored at San Jacinto?

146. Name the Texan who commanded the Flying Tigers. _____

147. Name the commander of Corregidor in the Philippines who surrendered to the Japanese during World War II. _____

148. How was General Earl Van Dorn, first Confederate commander of the Trans-Mississippi area, killed?

149. Where is the headquarters of the U.S. Fifth Army?

150. What Texas base hosted the III Armored Corps?

Answers

1. Conquistadores.
2. Hernan Cortes, who led conquistadors from Cuba to Mexico in 1519 and conquered Mexico.
3. Francisco Vásquez de Coronado, whose expedition moved northward across parts of New Mexico and Texas between 1540 and 1542. He found no gold but did discover Palo Duro Canyon and observed that the land would be suitable for grazing cattle.
4. The Comanche, called by some the "Lords of the Plains" once they acquired the horse.
5. Fort St. Louis, located near La Salle's landfall at Matagorda Bay. It was destroyed by Indians late in the 1680s after La Salle led a few of his men in search of other French settlements.
6. La Salle was murdered by his own men while seeking other French settlements. The exact site of the crime is disputed.
7. The *presidio*, a term that could refer to the garrison itself or to the place of their residence.
8. Teodoro de Croix, who was not especially successful.
9. San Antonio de Valero, established in 1718. Following their occupancy, the site was known thereafter as "The Alamo."
10. Filibusters, called *boucainiers* by the French, freebooters by the English, and *piratas* by the Spaniards.
11. Philip Nolan, who was killed in 1800 in a fight near the site of present-day Waco.
12. Ephraim Blackburn. Their sentence was commuted to having one in seven executed. Blackburn was

selected by lot when the men cast dice to determine who would be sacrificed.

13. General James Wilkinson.

14. Zebulon Pike, who sighted the peak named for him in Colorado and named the Great Desert of the Southwest.

15. The Neutral Ground, which separated the forces of the nations by fifty miles between the Sabine River and the Arroyo Hondo in Louisiana, and then north and south of that location along the river.

16. Lieutenant Augustus Magee.

17. Bernardo Gutierrez de Lara. Gutierrez and Magee were introduced by an American diplomat, leading to charges that the U.S. staged the invasion of Spanish lands.

18. General Joaquin de Arredondo, who then attempted to purge Texas of all Republicans.

19. Jean Lafitte, a French pirate who had earned a pardon from the U.S. for his aid in the defense of New Orleans against the British in 1815.

20. Dr. James Long of Natchez. After Secretary of State John Quincy Adams negotiated a treaty with Spain that barred western expansion beyond the Sabine and Red rivers, Long received support from other southerners who sought land where they would be free to follow their own lifestyle, including owning slaves.

21. Haden Edwards, formerly of Kentucky, worked with Stephen F. Austin to obtain colonization rights in Texas. Trouble in his grant area around Nacogdoches caused the government to cancel his grant, and he proclaimed his colony independent to retain it. He did not succeed.

22. General Manuel Mier y Terán, a member of the

Mexican "La Raza movement" that produced the
Law of April 6, 1830, cutting off American
immigration.

23. John (Juan) Davis Bradburn, an American in
Mexican service, who collected taxes and enforced
other laws that irritated American settlers and
Mexican state officials alike.

24. José de las Piedras, a colonel in the Mexican Army.
Loyal to Terán and the Centralists, defused the
Disturbance at Anáhuac, then caused one in
Nacogdoches.

25. When Piedras returned to Nacogdoches, he
ordered civilians in the area to turn in their guns;
their refusal resulted in the Battle of Nacogdoches
on August 2 and 3, 1832.

26. Austin attempted to bring a cannon to Anáhuac to
free William B. Travis and Patrick Jack, who were
captives of Bradburn.

27. The Turtle Bayou Resolutions, basically a pledge of
continued loyalty to the legal constitution and
opposition to Centralists such as Bradburn, whom
they accused of violating the Constitution of 1824.

28. Colonel José Antonio Mexia, a supporter of Santa
Anna in the north of Mexico, visited Texas and was
persuaded by Stephen F. Austin to regard the
"Disturbances" as being in support of Santa Anna's
revolution. It was a pretense by Santa Anna that he
favored states' rights.

29. General Martín Perfecto de Cós, who
headquartered at Monclova with the intention of
making that city the state capital. Cós also sent
troops to various sites in Texas.

30. William B. Travis, who had been involved in the
trouble in Anáhuac in 1832. Since then he had

moved to San Felipe and had become involved with the War Party, a group that advocated armed resistance to the central Mexican government. Travis accepted command of this ad hoc unit and captured Tenorio's command, re-igniting the trouble that then led to Santa Anna's march north with a large army to suppress the rebellion in Texas.

31. At Gonzales, where General Cós dispatched a group of soldiers to seize a cannon in October 1835. The community defended their cannon successfully.

32. The words "Come And Take It" appeared with an outline drawing of a cannon on a field of white.

33. Stephen F. Austin, leader of the Americans then in Texas; he was not really suited for the role and accepted a diplomatic assignment from the Consultation before the Battle of San Antonio.

34. Benjamin Milam, although command of Austin's "Army of the People" had devolved upon Edward Burleson when Austin left on a diplomatic mission to the U.S. When the battle for San Antonio began, Milam commanded the assault and Burleson commanded the reserve. Milam was killed in the fighting.

35. Francis (Frank) Johnson accepted the invitation of Dr. James Grant to join him in a venture to sack the Mexican city of Matamoros.

36. Colonel James C. Neill, who constantly complained to the interim government of Governor Henry Smith about his lack of men and supplies to defend the city.

37. Colonel James Fannin, or Fanning, the only

commander in the Texas defense forces with any formal military training.

38. William Barret Travis, who was ordered to San Antonio with as many recruits as possible to assist Neill; he arrived with fewer than thirty men, then became commander of the Texas "regulars" when Neill took leave.

39. James Bowie, who had been ordered to San Antonio to raze the city but remained instead to defend it.

40. Green Jamison, who supervised the establishment of gun emplacements and shoring up the walls.

41. "Dequello"; said to be a signal of no quarter, it was actually a standard bugle call of Mexican cavalry.

42. The precise number remains in doubt, with estimates ranging from 183 to 187.

43. Louis, or Moses, Rose claims this distinction; his story was not broadly known until Frederick Zuber published an account of it in the *Texas Almanac* in 1873. Zuber, however, was not an eye-witness to any of the events involving Rose and much of the story remains unproven.

44. David Crockett came to Texas after losing his seat in Congress, either intending to make a permanent home or to use it as a base of a new political career. He was killed at the Alamo. There is controversy about the way Crockett died—some believe that he perished fighting, others think he surrendered when resistance was futile and was executed.

45. Sam Houston, and he did so twice: first when the Consultation met in November 1835, but he had difficulty finding an army to lead; second when the group met in March 1836. This time Houston found

troops at Gonzales awaiting orders to assist at the Alamo. He later led this army in the San Jacinto campaign.

46. Colonel Sidney Sherman, who remained with Houston and shared command at the Battle of San Jacinto.

47. Erastus ("Deaf") Smith, who was also a poet.

48. Fannin's troops at Goliad were captured by Mexican forces led by General José Urrea and executed by order of Santa Anna; only a few survived.

49. The Runaway Scrape, a terrible experience for the refugees who abandoned homes and furnishings in a wild rush to safety.

50. Two cannons, known as the "Twin Sisters," were used to open the Mexican line at San Jacinto.

51. The Texans' flag was a plain white shield with a single, five-pointed star. It contained the words, *Ubi Libertas Habit Ibi Nostra Patria Est* (where liberty lives, there is my homeland).

52. "Will You Come To The Bower I Have Shaded For You," played on a fife accompanied by a drummer.

53. General Edmund Gaines, commander of the frontier forces, used militia from several states to secure the border and also to provide support for refugees from and in eastern Texas.

54. The Treaty of Velasco, signed on May 14, 1836, by Santa Anna and interim President David G. Burnet; among other things, the treaty provided for all Mexican troops in Texas to be withdrawn to Mexico.

55. Burton's cavalrymen were called "Horse Marines" after they captured a Mexican ship at Copano Bay on June 2, 1836.

56. Commodore Edwin Moore. The Texas Navy controlled Gulf waters and prevented Santa Anna from receiving supplies by sea as planned. During the Republic, President Mirabeau Lamar sent Moore to assist Yucatan rebels in harassing the Mexicans; when Moore refused to return, President Sam Houston branded him a pirate and invited the world's navies to sink his ships.

57. Texas soldiers received one headright, or 640 acres, plus one bounty grant of 320 acres for each three months of service.

58. Felix Huston, who enjoyed the confidence of most soldiers, challenged Johnston to a duel.

59. Houston furloughed, but did not discharge, all but 600 soldiers in the Texas army.

60. Lamar unsuccessfully sent men to Santa Fe for this purpose.

61. General Zachary Taylor, "Old Rough And Ready," commanded there by order of President James K. Polk. Clashes in the area between the Nueces River and the Rio Grande gave both nations a reason to commence war.

62. General Winfield Scott, "Old Fuss And Feathers," diverted men and supplies from Taylor for his invasion of Mexico, which stalled Taylor and enabled Scott to reach Mexico City first.

63. *Los Diablos Tejanos,* or the Devil Texans, who fought with a zeal that convinced all observers that they still wanted revenge for the massacres at the Alamo and Goliad.

64. General David E. Twiggs, who commanded troops headquartered in San Antonio and manning posts on a line from Fort Worth southward.

65. Hood's Texas Brigade, named for its first

commander, General John Bell Hood. They fought primarily in the Eastern Theatre of the Civil War.

66. Terry's Texas Rangers, named for General B. F. Terry; they retained that name throughout the war even after Terry was killed.

67. General Felix Houston Robertson.

68. General Paul Octave Hebert, of Louisiana, who did not get along well with Texans.

69. General John Bankhead Magruder, of Virginia, who proved to be more popular with Texans than did Hebert.

70. "Rip," for the R.I.P. (rest in peace) conclusion of casualty lists in his battle reports.

71. General Edmund Kirby Smith of Florida.

72. Colonel John R. Baylor, who chased U.S. troops out of New Mexico in 1861, then was made governor of the Territory, a position he did not hold for long.

73. General H. H. Sibley, who had been successful in earlier actions; he eventually lost command because of failure and a fondness for alcohol.

74. "The Yellow Rose of Texas," written in 1853.

75. Cottonclads because General Magruder lined the decks with bales of cotton as cover for his men.

76. At Sabine Pass. On September 8, 1863, the U.S. Navy attempted to land forces commanded by General Nathaniel P. Banks on the upper end of Sabine Lake near the Louisiana border. Dowling's gunners disabled two vessels, blocking the channel, and the invasion forces withdrew.

77. The Battle of Mansfield, fought on April 8, 1864, in northwestern Louisiana.

78. On June 19, 1865, General Gordon Granger arrived in Galveston and proclaimed the war over in Texas.

79. The Battle of Palmito Ranch, fought on May 11, 1865, by Confederate forces commanded by John S. Ford and U.S. troops commanded by Colonel David Branson.
80. General Wesley Merritt.
81. General George Armstrong Custer served for a time in Austin. He headquartered at the state school for the deaf, where, it is claimed, Custer learned the sign language he used on the plains before his death at the Little Bighorn.
82. Military District #5. Texas was considered a subprovince of that district, not a state of the Union.
83. General Philip Sheridan, who said that if he owned Texas and Hell, he would live in Hell and rent out Texas; commanders of the district who succeeded Sheridan before Reconstruction ended include Generals George H. Thomas, Winfield Scott Hancock, and E. R. Canby.
84. James N. Norris, who instituted regular patrols that proved unsuccessful; later J. E. McCord assumed command and was more successful with sporadic and therefore less predictable patrols. Finally, James W. Throckmorton led the regiment after 1864.
85. The Battle of Adobe Walls, fought mostly by Union troops against Plains Indians.
86. Buffalo Soldiers; they provided excellent service on the Indian frontier.
87. The "Quaker Peace Policy." Grant hoped that by sending Quakers as agents to the Plains Indians, the agents' benevolent beliefs would help to pacify the tribes.
88. The Salt Creek Massacre, in which an army

paymaster and escorts were killed in 1871. Generals William T. Sherman and Randolph Marcy were with the party but had moved on ahead, thus saving their lives.

89. Satanta, who was captured by General Sherman; he was killed when he leaped from a second-story window at the penitentiary.

90. Colonel Ranald S. Mackenzie, who met the commands of Nelson A. Miles, William Price, John Davidson, and George Buel in a pincer maneuver at Palo Duro Canyon. The majority of the hostile Indians were captured, thus ending most Indian raids in Texas. What kept the Indians on the reservation, however, was not U.S. soldiers but the elimination of the buffalo from the plains by hunters.

91. The Rough Riders, officially the 1st U.S. Volunteers, were commanded by Colonel Leonard Wood with future president Theodore Roosevelt also holding a position in its officer corps. Not all the Rough Riders were Texans, but Texas did have strong representation in the ranks.

92. Francisco ("Pancho") Villa was the raider. Other revolutionaries lived in Texas in exile and planned revolutions against the Mexican government from the Lone Star State. They included the Flores Magón brothers, Gilberto Guerrero, and Francisco Madero.

93. John J. Pershing, also called "Black Jack" because of his previous leadership of black troops.

94. The Zimmerman Note Incident, which involved a communication from German Foreign Minister Arthur Zimmerman proposing an alliance with Mexico in the event of war and promising Mexico

the return of all territory—from Texas to California—taken by the U.S.

95. E. M. House of Austin, the president's closest advisor during his first administration and for part of his second administration, traveled to many European nations trying to prevent war. House later advised Wilson on a post-war peace plan, including the founding of the League of Nations.

96. John Nance Garner of Uvalde, later speaker of the house and a two-term vice president of the United States.

97. Thomas Connally, who later served in the U.S. Senate and also sponsored the resolution that permitted the U.S. to join the United Nations.

98. The creation of the War Risk Insurance Board to provide life insurance for American servicemen.

99. Benny D. Foulois, who established his base at San Antonio because the area averaged over 200 days of good flying weather annually. Foulois set the first distance record in a military aeroplane, flying from Laredo to Eagle Pass. He also accompanied Pershing to Europe as a member of the First Aero Squadron.

100. Eventually 989,571 Texans registered for the draft; approximately 200,000 draftees and volunteers actually served; 5,171 Texans died while in service, although only about 2,700 were killed in battle—the remainder died of disease, especially influenza.

101. Senator Thomas Connally.

102. At the beginning of the conflict, San Antonio was the headquarters of the Third Army; during the war it became the headquarters of the Fourth Army as well and was the training site for 1.25 million American service personnel.

103. Randolph Field in San Antonio; that city also hosted Brooks, Kelly, and Lackland fields. Texas had forty airfields in all, where over 200,000 pilots, bombardiers, and gunners received training.

104. Approximately 750,000, of whom 23,022 died while in service: 15,764 in the army and 7,258 in other services.

105. Thirty-six.

106. Audie Murphy of Farmersville; Murphy was turned down by most services because of age and slight build, but entered the army at the age of seventeen and became a hero in the European Theater.

107. Samuel Dealey of Dallas County.

108. Doris Miller of McLennan County, a ship's steward during the Japanese attack on Pearl Harbor who shot down an enemy airplane with an anti-aircraft gun with which he had had no training.

109. 150.

110. Dwight David Eisenhower, born in Denison. His family moved to Kansas when he was a child. After Eisenhower entered West Point, he became a citizen of the world, eventually rising to president of the United States. During the war he served as supreme commander of allied forces in North Africa and in Europe.

111. Twelve.

112. Chester Nimitz, from Fredericksburg, who became commander-in-chief of the Pacific Fleet during World War II.

113. Oveta Culp Hobby, who commanded the Women's Auxiliary (later Army) Corps.

114. Twenty-nine; they hosted prisoners from the Axis nations—especially Germans—who were employed

in various industries doing the work of Texans then in the service.

115. The Thirty-sixth Division, a National Guard unit before its activation, fought in North Africa, Italy, and Germany, and served as an occupation force after the war.

116. d. El Paso

117. k. Brackettville

118. g. Killeen

119. j. San Antonio

120. f. Tyler

121. h. Austin

122. i. Texarkana

123. c. Galveston

124. a. Wichita Falls

125. b. Houston

126. Popular culture insists that their flag was the Mexican tricolor with the numbers "1824" imposed upon it, but the only battle flag Mexican forces acknowledge capturing at the Alamo was that of one of the units of the defenders known as the New Orleans Grays.

127. Mostly the issue of the location of the state capital. After President Mirabeau Lamar located the capital at Austin, his successor, Sam Houston, refused to serve there and sent for the state archives, but the citizens of Austin literally fought to retain their claim as the capital city by offering armed resistance. They prevailed.

128. General José Urrea defeated Texans commanded by Dr. James Grant in this action of March 2, 1836.

129. Sam Houston, designated by the First Consultation; as well as James Grant, Francis Johnson, and James Fannin, all designated at one time or another by

the council of the interim government. In the confusion, Houston quit the field and traveled to East Texas to negotiate a treaty with the Cherokee Indians, but was asked to command Texas forces again by the Second Consultation.

130. James Butler Bonham, who made several exits from the Alamo to carry messages for William B. Travis and always returned.

131. General José Urrea captured the forces commanded by Colonel James Fannin after this battle on March 19 and 20, 1836.

132. In 1838, Vincente Cordova, a *Tejano*, led a rebellion against the Republic of Texas in support of Mexico's goal of reclaiming the territory.

133. Texas Rangers and Comanche Indians clashed over white captives held by the Comanche on March 19, 1840, near San Antonio.

134. The unit commanded by Lieutenant Dick Dowling at the Battle of Sabine Pass, September 8, 1863, during the Civil War. Officially, they were Company F, Heavy Artillery.

135. During the Siege of San Antonio, on November 26, 1835, desperate Texas forces attacked a Mexican supply train, only to discover that the train was carrying hay for Mexican horses.

136. Albert Sidney Johnston, a West Point graduate who came to Texas during the Republic. Later he reentered the U.S. Army and commanded during the Mormon War, then joined the Confederate Army in 1861.

137. The Battle of San Jacinto, April 21, 1836, in which Texas forces commanded by General Sam Houston defeated Mexican troops commanded by Santa Anna.

138. Robert E. Lee, later the commander of the Confederate Army of Northern Virginia during the Civil War.

139. Texan forces commanded by Thomas J. Rusk and Kelsey Douglass defeated Cherokee Indians led by Chief Bowles, resulting in the Cherokee being forced to leave Texas for Indian Territory.

140. Adolphus Sterne, a merchant in Nacogdoches, traveled to Louisiana and recruited two companies known as New Orleans Grays. He did so at a personal expense of $990, a considerable sum at the time; one unit served at the Alamo and another at Goliad.

141. U.S. forces commanded by General Zachary Taylor defeated Mexican troops commanded by General Mariano Arista at this battle near Brownsville on May 8, 1846, during the Mexican War.

142. General Lawrence Sullivan ("Sul") Ross; he also served as governor of Texas, 1887-1891.

143. A dispute over rights to salt deposits in the vicinity of Guadalupe Peak near El Paso during the late 1860s; the conflict was so severe that it led to the establishment of Fort Bliss so troops would be available to maintain order.

144. A war-like disturbance in DeWitt County between the Joshua Taylor family and E. J. Davis' state police. It began when Deputy Sheriff William Sutton killed Buck Taylor on December 24, 1868. This led to several clashes between partisans of the two sides, and the feud lasted until 1874.

145. The *USS Texas*, commissioned on March 12, 1914; the *Texas* served during World Wars I and II in the Pacific and Atlantic oceans and took part in five invasions in North Africa, southern and northern

France, and at Iwo Jima and Okinawa. She was placed in permanent harbor at San Jacinto on April 21, 1948, and was restored in 1990 and 1991.

146. Claire Lee Chennault, born in Commerce in 1890, commanded this irregular unit in the China Theater during World War II.

147. Jonathan Mayhew Wainwright, who assumed command when General Douglas MacArthur left for Australia; he was held prisoner-of-war by the Japanese for over three years, but was present on the USS *Missouri* when Japan surrendered. Wainwright lived in San Antonio during his retirement.

148. Van Dorn was shot by a Dr. Peters, allegedly for trifling with the man's wife.

149. Fort Sam Houston in San Antonio.

150. Fort Hood, located at Killeen between Austin and Waco.

7

Do Texans Play Any Games?

The answer is obvious. There is *football*. Friday-Nite Follies or Madness—it goes by different names—starts the weekend for hundreds of thousands of Texans in the fall. On Saturday—after the Friday night high school contests—they watch their favorite college team, or even the telecast of a game between two universities they have never attended. Many both attend *and* watch a game on TV. And the preacher better hurry his sermon on Sunday if the Cowboys or Oilers play in the East and the kickoff is at 11:30 A.M., CST. It is the Lord's blessing if one of these teams has an early game and the other doesn't begin their game until mid-afternoon. Football appeals to Texans because it represents competition and a little controlled violence—both long traditions in the Lone Star State.

The majority of Texans are sports-minded, and sports

play a significant role in the mosaic of Texas culture. So play along. It will not be possible to cover every sport, but something is included—from golf to boxing—that will interest everyone.

Football

Let's start off with an easy exercise. Fill in the mascot's name for the football (and other) teams of the Southwest Conference universities listed:

1. The University of Texas _____
2. Texas A&M University _____
3. Baylor University _____
4. Texas Christian University _____
5. Southern Methodist University _____
6. University of Houston _____
7. Texas Tech University _____
8. Rice University _____

There is much more to Texas college football than just the Southwest Conference, so for the really dedicated, press on with more mascots:

9. Angelo State University _____
10. Lamar University (this school dropped football recently, but still—what is their mascot?) _____

11. Sam Houston State University _____
12. Southwest Texas State University _____
13. Stephen F. Austin State University _____
14. Texas Southern University _____
15. The University of North Texas _____
16. The University of Texas at El Paso _____

17. Sul Ross State University _____

Bonus: give yourself an extra point if you know the mascot of Austin College.

Until recently, intercollegiate athletics was largely an all-male endeavor. Now many of these schools also have full-scale athletic programs for women. Try just a few of the universities, this time giving the name of mascots of teams for women:

18. The University of Texas _____
19. Stephen F. Austin State University _____
20. Wayland Baptist College _____
21. Tarleton State University _____
22. Sam Houston State University _____

Now let's separate the fair-weather fans from the truly dedicated.

23. The first intercollegiate football game played in Texas involved teams from what schools? _____

_____

24. Who won the game? _____
25. The Southwest Conference was organized in what year? _____
26. The first two Texans to be named All-America football players (they played for Centre College in Kentucky) were? _____
27. Who was the first Texan who became a first-team All-America player for a Texas team? _____

_____

28. Which Texas team was the first to play in the Rose Bowl? _____

29. What Texas player won the Maxwell Trophy his sophomore year, the Heisman Trophy as a junior, and was Sportsman of the Year when a senior? ____

30. Name the six Texas players who have won the Heisman Trophy (up to 1991). _____
31. and? _____
32. and? _____
33. and? _____
34. and? _____
35. and? _____
36. Two of the Heisman Trophy winners attended the same high school in Dallas. Name the school. ____

37. What Texas player holds the current (1993) NCAA record for passing 690 yards in a single game? ____

38. When Doak Walker could not play for SMU against Notre Dame in 1949 because of injury, who replaced him, then ran and passed for 261 yards, and averaged 48 yards on punt returns? _____

39. The coach who led his Longhorn team to eleven conference championships, three national championships, and sixteen bowl games was? ____

40. Who was the college coach credited with inventing the Wishbone-T formation? _____

41. Which Texas college won six NAIA national championships in football? _____
42. And who coached the teams that won those championships? _____
43. In 1959 and 1960, what North Texas State

University (now The University of North Texas) athletes were selected as All-America? _____

44. and? _____
45. What two SMU players became known as the "Pony Express?" _____
46. and? _____
47. Which school from the Southwest Conference resigned to join the Southeast Conference in 1990?

48. What is the only Texas school that has been handed the NCAA's "Death Penalty" (suspension from play) for rules violations? _____
49. When Doak Walker became a Detroit Lion, he joined his high school teammate who had played at The University of Texas. A quarterback, he was?

50. Founded in 1952, the first professional football team in Texas was known as? _____
51. This team, unsuccessful in Texas, moved to what city and played under what name? _____
52. Who were the two "Texas millionaires" who founded the American Football League? _____

53. and? _____
54. Their teams were known as? _____
55. and? _____
56. Which team won the first two AFL championships? _____

57. In the third AFL championship game the Houston and Dallas teams established what record that still stands? _____
58. A second professional team came to Dallas in 1960

as a franchise of the National Football League. It is known as what? _____

59. Its principal owner, its general manager (later the team president), and its coach were: principal owner? _____

60. general manager, later president? _____

61. coach? _____

62. What player was known as "the fastest man alive?" _____

63. The championship game this team lost to the Green Bay Packers in the 13-degree weather of Wisconsin is known as? _____

64. Through 1991, how many times did the Dallas team play in the Super Bowl under its original coach? _____

65. How many of those Super Bowl games did they win? _____

66. This Dallas team drafted its most successful quarterback, Roger Staubach, after he had played for what collegiate team? _____

67. This Dallas team's personal manager, the "recruiter with a computer" was? _____

68. The team's first owner sold the franchise in the mid-1980s to a consortium headed by? _____

69. In 1989, his group sold the franchise to what Arkansas businessman? _____

70. This new owner replaced most of the office and field personnel. Who did he name as the Dallas team's new coach? _____

71. What former player with Houston's team played professional football over four decades? _____

72. The Houston team employed ten head coaches in

their first fifteen years. Who did they hire as coach in 1975? _____

73. What Houston player was known as the "Tyler Rose?" _____

74. Who was the Houston coach who dressed in black and left tickets at the gate for the deceased Elvis Presley? _____

75. What was the name of Houston's team in the United States Football League? _____

Bonus Question: this one is a little tougher, so don't count off if you miss it, but give yourself a bonus point if you know who coached the Dallas Texans in the Arena Football League when Mitchell Ward was the team's primary running back.

Baseball

Although some Texas sports fans find that their calendar has only two seasons—football season and the time until the next football season—other sports are alive and well in the Lone Star State. And many baseball fans view the year in much the same way, merely substituting "baseball" for "football" in their calendar.

Baseball has been an important sport in Texas for more than 100 years. Texans have played the game in leagues ranging from the American and National Leagues (majors) to a number of so-called "minor" leagues. There also have been industrial leagues (a relative of this writer swears he kept his job during the Depression because he could play the game well) and, when all else fails, the old sand-lot variety of ball or just plain catch whiles away the hours.

See what you remember about baseball's impact on Texas.

Texas League

In 1950, the Texas League included the following teams. Name the team that played for the town listed:

76. Beaumont _____

77. Fort Worth _____

78. Tulsa _____

79. San Antonio _____

80. Dallas _____

81. Oklahoma City _____

82. Shreveport _____

83. Houston _____

As is suggested by this list, the "Texas League" included teams from other states. For only fifteen years of its century or so of existence was it composed exclusively of teams from Texas, and over that time, thirty-eight cities outside Texas have been members of the league. Also, many Texas cities had teams in the league at one time or another. Match a city with a team name in the following list. There is an extra team to give you a handicap on guessing:

84. Albuquerque, New Mexico
85. Alexandria, Louisiana
86. Corsicana
87. Denison
88. Galveston
89. Jackson, Mississippi
90. Lafayette, Louisiana
91. Little Rock, Arkansas
92. Memphis, Tennessee
93. Temple

a. Aces
b. Tigers
c. Hunters
d. Drillers
e. Blues
f. Boll Weevils
g. Travellers
h. Mets
i. Buccaneers
j. Oilers
k. Dukes

Identify the following major-league players with the minor-league teams for which they played in Texas:

94. Carl Hubbell _____
95. Red Murff _____
96. Dizzy Dean _____
97. Hank Greenburg _____
98. Carl Erskine _____
99. Fernando Valenzuela _____

Now for some specifics:

100. Jim Turner, who played for several Texas league teams, was known by what nickname? _____

101. Houston was the first southern city to achieve major-league status. What was the name of its first "major" team? _____

102. The team's name was changed to what when it moved into a new stadium in 1964? _____

103. This team traded what star player to the Cincinnati Reds, where he became an All-Star, the league's Most Valuable Player, and Hall of Fame honoree?

104. They also traded what star pitcher to the Texas Rangers? _____

105. This performer holds what two major-league pitching records? _____

106. and? _____

107. The Dallas-Fort Worth area acquired what franchise and renamed the team Texas Rangers? _____

108. What Texas-born player was known as "The Gray Eagle" when he played for the Cleveland Indians?

109. What Texas-born player is regarded as baseball's best right-handed hitter? _____

110. Who was the Texas-born player who returned to play after the loss of a leg as a result of a hunting accident? _____

111. Roger Clemens, Cy Young Award-winning pitcher for the Boston Red Sox, played for what Texas university team? _____

112. Duke Snider played for what Texas professional team? _____

113. Texas League champions won what playoff series

between first-division finishers at the end of the season? _____

Basketball

Sports historian James Pohl says that "until recently basketball in Texas might have been aptly described as the game one fooled around with between the football and baseball seasons." Basketball now has a permanent and prominent place in schoolboy, collegiate, and professional sports.

114. Who coached the Texas Longhorns to the National Invitational Tournament Championship in 1978? __

115. Elvin Hayes played for what Texas team? _____

116. The University of Texas Lady Longhorn coach who led her team to a perfect season in 1986 was? _____

117. Sue Gunter, later coach at LSU, founded and coached what Texas women's team to Top Ten status? _____

118. What two college teams played in the Astrodome before the largest crowd to see such a game to that date? _____

119. What was the first professional basketball team in Texas? _____

120. This franchise moved to San Antonio in 1973 and played under what name? _____

121. Their star player during the 1970s, who had played college ball in Virginia, was? _____

122. Houston acquired an NBA franchise in 1971 from San Diego. In Houston, the team's name became?

123. Akeem Olajouwan, the University of Houston and Houston professional basketball player, came from what country? _____

124. The Dallas-based NBA franchise is known by what team name? _____

Other Sports

What do you know about Golf?

125. What Texas school did *Golf Digest* call "the Notre Dame of Golf?" _____

126. This school produced the winner of the Texas Open, the Tournament of Champions, and the PGA in 1967. He is? _____

127. From Fort Worth, what Texas golfer won forty-nine PGA tournaments in the 1930s and 1940s? _____

128. What golfer from Houston is a three-time winner of the Masters'? _____

129. What Texas golfer was the first Mexican-American to win a PGA tournament? _____

130. What Texas golfer was the first black to play in the Masters'? _____

131. What Texas golfer won four USGA Open tournaments, two Masters', two PGA tournaments, and the British Open after being severely injured in an auto accident? _____

132. Who has been Texas' most outstanding woman golfer? _____

133. What tournament played in the Lone Star State is even older than the Masters'? _____

134. The Colonial Invitational Tournament is played in what Texas city? _____

135. The Byron Nelson Tournament is played in what Texas city? _____

136. In what city is the Legends of Golf Tournament played? _____

Boxing?

137. The group historically associated with promoting boxing among youth and other amateurs is? _____

138. In 1967, Muhammad Ali successfully defended his heavyweight title against what contender from Dallas? _____

139. Ali also successfully defended his title against what two fighters in the Astrodome in 1966 and 1967?

140. and? _____

141. What Texan won the gold medal in Olympic competition in the heavyweight division in 1968?

142. He won the heavyweight championship of the world in 1972 by defeating whom? _____

143. Who was the first black Texan to win the heavyweight championship? _____

144. Who was the legendary boxing promoter who was born in Sherman in 1890? _____

Soccer?

145. In 1967, what Dallas businessman helped to found the North American Soccer League? _____

146. What son of a Southwest Conference and National Football League player became an outstanding soccer player in Dallas? _____

147. What is the team name of the Dallas franchise in the Major Soccer League? _____

148. What Southwest Conference team produced seven All-America soccer players and participated in NCAA playoffs eight times? _____

149. The international professional soccer championship competition is known as? _____

This 'n That

150. In what decade did professional hockey make its debut in Texas? _____

151. The Houston franchise in the World Hockey League during the 1970s was known as? _____

152. What Texas team won the Central Hockey League championship in 1979? _____

153. Doubtless the most famous hockey player associated with a Texas team was? _____

154. What Texas track-and-field athlete won an Olympic gold medal for the shotput? _____

155. What Houston Olympian was noted for the broadjump and sprint competition? _____

156. Who is the best known Texas-born jockey? _____

157. Who is Houston's favorite son in auto racing? _____

158. Why would Southwest Conference schools prefer to play in the Cotton Bowl on New Year's Day?

159. The Texan who won the NFL's Most Valuable Player Award as a kicker with the Washington Redskins is? _____

160. The Chicago Cub's favorite Texan and homerun hitter is? _____

Bonus: Who won designation as Most Valuable Player in the Texas League in 1950? _____

Answers

1. The University of Texas Longhorns.
2. Texas A&M University Aggies.
3. Baylor University Bears.
4. Texas Christian University (TCU) Horned Frogs.
5. Southern Methodist University (SMU) Mustangs.
6. The University of Houston Cougars.
7. Texas Tech University Red Raiders.
8. Rice University Owls.
9. Angelo State University Rams.
10. Lamar University Cardinals.
11. Sam Houston State University BearKats.
12. Southwest Texas State University BobCats.
13. Stephen F. Austin State University Lumberjacks.
14. Texas Southern University Tigers.
15. The University of North Texas Eagles.
16. The University of Texas at El Paso Miners.
17. Sul Ross State University Lobos.
    Bonus Answer: Austin College Kangaroos.
18. The University of Texas Lady Longhorns.
19. Stephen F. Austin State University LadyJacks.
20. Wayland Baptist College Flying Queens.
21. Tarleton State University TexAnns.
22. Sam Houston State University LadyKats.
23. The first intercollegiate football game was played in Austin in 1894. Texas A&M College and the University of Texas fielded teams.
24. The University of Texas, 38-0.
25. The Southwest Conference was organized in 1914.
26. The first Texans to be named All-America were Alvin "Bo" McMillan and James "Red" Weaver, who played for the Praying Colonels of Centre College in Kentucky.

27. The first Texan named a first-team All-America while playing for a college located in Texas was Darrell Lester. He played center at TCU.
28. SMU beat Stanford, 7-0, in 1935.
29. Doak Walker of SMU, who wore jersey number 37, played varsity ball from 1947 to 1949.
30. Davey O'Brien, TCU.
31. John Kimbrough, Texas A&M.
32. Doak Walker, SMU.
33. John David Crow, Texas A&M.
34. Earl Campbell, The University of Texas.
35. Andre Ware, University of Houston.
36. Davey O'Brien, TCU, and Tim Brown, Notre Dame, attended Woodrow Wilson High School in Dallas.
37. Matt Vogler of TCU, second-string quarterback who played because starter Leon Clay had a broken thumb; David Klingler of the University of Houston threw for 563 yards in the same game—and won!
38. Kyle Rote, who had played for Thomas Jefferson High School in San Antonio. The next year he was named to the All-America team.
39. Darrell Royal at the University of Texas.
40. Emory Bellard, an assistant coach under Darrell Royal at the University of Texas, and later head coach at Texas A&M.
41. Texas A&I at Kingsville.
42. Gil Steinke, whose career record is 182 wins, 61 loses, and 4 ties.
43. Abner Haynes in 1959.
44. Joe Greene, later known as Mean Joe Greene, in 1960.
45. Craig James.
46. Eric Dickerson.

47. The University of Arkansas.
48. SMU, as a result of illegal payments to players and other violations known to coaches, administrators, and trustees.
49. Bobby Layne, who had played at Highland Park High School near Dallas.
50. Dallas Texans.
51. Baltimore Colts, now Indianapolis Colts.
52. Lamar Hunt
53. K. S. "Bud" Adams.
54. Dallas Texans.
55. Houston Oilers.
56. Houston Oilers.
57. They played the longest official football game on record—seventeen minutes into sudden death overtime. Dallas won on Tommy Booker's field goal, 20-17.
58. Dallas Cowboys.
59. Clint Murchison, Jr.
60. Tex Schramm.
61. Tom Landry.
62. "Bullet" Bob Hayes.
63. The game was known as the "Ice Bowl."
64. Five.
65. Two.
66. The United States Naval Academy. Staubach was graduated in 1964 but did not report to the Cowboys until 1969 because of his service obligation.
67. Gil Brandt.
68. "Bum" Bright.
69. Jerry Jones.
70. Jimmy Johnson.
71. George Blanda, who earlier had played for the

Chicago Bears and finished his career as a kicker and backup quarterback for the Oakland Raiders.

72. A. A. "Bum" Phillips.
73. Earl Campbell of Tyler. He won the Heisman Trophy while playing at the University of Texas in 1978 and was inducted into professional football's Hall of Fame in 1991.
74. Jerry Glanville, who left in 1990 to coach the Atlanta Falcons.
75. Houston Gunslingers.
    Bonus answer: Ernie Stauntner, formerly an assistant coach with the Dallas Cowboys.
76. Beaumont Exporters.
77. Fort Worth Panthers, or "Cats."
78. Tulsa Oilers.
79. San Antonio Missions.
80. Dallas Eagles.
81. Oklahoma City Indians.
82. Shreveport Sports.
83. Houston Buffalos, or Buffs.
84. k. Albuquerque Dukes.
85. a. Alexandria Aces.
86. j. Corsicana Oilers.
87. b. Denison Tigers.
88. i. Galveston Buccaneers.
89. h. Jackson Mets.
90. d. Lafayette Drillers.
91. g. Little Rock Travellers.
92. e. Memphis Blues.
93. f. Temple Boll Weevils.
94. Carl Hubbell played for the Beaumont Exporters and the New York Giants.
95. "Red" Murff played for the Dallas Eagles and the Milwaukee Braves.

96. Dizzy Dean played for the Houston Buffs and the St. Louis Cardinals.
97. Hank Greenburg played for the Beaumont Exporters and the Detroit Lions.
98. Carl Erskine played for the Fort Worth Cats and the Brooklyn Dodgers.
99. Fernando Valenzuela played for the San Antonio and Los Angeles Dodgers.
100. Turner was called "Milkman" Jim Turner.
101. Texas' first major-league team was the Houston Colt .45s.
102. The Houston franchise changed its team's name to the Astros when they began playing in the new Astrodome.
103. Houston traded Joe Morgan to the Cincinnati Reds.
104. Nolan Ryan.
105. Ryan played for the Mets, Angels, Astros, and Texas Rangers, and holds major-league records for most strikeouts (over 5000).
106. Most no-hit games (seven through the 1991 season), among others.
107. The Texas Rangers franchise was moved from Washington, D.C., where the team was known as the Senators.
108. Tris Speaker, from Hubbard, near Waco.
109. Rogers Hornsby, born on his father's ranch near Winters, played for the St. Louis Cardinals. His lifetime batting average is .358, second only to Ty Cobb's average of .367. Hornsby batted over .400 in three years during his career.
110. Monty Stratton, who pitched for the Chicago White Sox. Actor James Stewart portrayed Stratton

in a motion picture based on the ballplayer's life and brief comeback in baseball.

111. Roger Clemens played for the University of Texas Longhorns.

112. Duke Snider played in Fort Worth.

113. The Texas League adopted a plan devised by Frank Shaughnessy for the International League to increase fan interest at the end of the season. It called for the first- and fourth-place teams and the second- and third-place teams to play each other, and the winners of each pair to play for the championship.

114. A. E. "Abe" Lemons.

115. The University of Houston Cougars.

116. Jody Conradt.

117. Stephen F. Austin State University LadyJacks.

118. The University of Houston and UCLA played before 52,693 fans. Houston won, 71-69.

119. Dallas Chaparrals, in the American Basketball Association, in 1967.

120. The San Antonio Spurs.

121. George "Ice Man" Gervin.

122. The Houston Rockets.

123. Akeem Olajouwan came from Nigeria.

124. The Dallas Mavericks.

125. North Texas State University, now The University of North Texas, which won four consecutive NCAA national championships, 1949–1952.

126. Don January.

127. Byron Nelson.

128. Jimmy Demaret.

129. Lee Trevino.

130. Lee Elder.

131. Ben Hogan.
132. Mildred "Babe" Didrikson Zaharias.
133. The Texas Open, sometimes called the San Antonio-Texas Open.
134. Fort Worth.
135. Dallas.
136. Austin.
137. The Golden Gloves.
138. Zora Foley.
139. Cleveland Williams.
140. Ernie Terrell.
141. George Foreman.
142. "Smokin' Joe" Frazier, with a knockout in the second round.
143. Jack Johnson.
144. George "Tex" Rickard, who promoted Jack Dempsey's fights (among others), in Madison Square Garden.
145. Lamar Hunt.
146. Kyle Rote, Jr.
147. Dallas Sidekicks.
148. Southern Methodist University.
149. The World Cup.
150. Professional hockey began in Texas in the 1940s.
151. The Houston Aeros.
152. The Fort Worth Texans, who defeated the Dallas Black Hawks.
153. Gordie Howe, who skated for the Houston Aeros; he had two sons playing on the same team.
154. Randy Matson, of Texas A&M, who also won three NCAA championships in this event.
155. Carl Lewis.
156. Willie Shoemaker.

157. A. J. Foyt.
158. Because the Southwest Conference football champion plays in the Cotton Bowl each year.
159. Mark Moseley.
160. Ernie Banks.

Bonus Answer: Gil McDougal, second baseman, who then advanced to the New York Yankees.

8

What Does That Mean?

Time to define some terms. Historians often speak in a kind of verbal shorthand. "Shortcuts" probably is a better way to state the case. But a lot of terms are thrown around in both written and spoken forms, and reader-hearers may not have any idea what they mean. This exercise obviously can't be all-inclusive, but here are some obvious terms, acronyms, etc., that relate to Texas history.

Define the following:

1. Carpetbagger _____
2. Scalawag _____
3. Hoodlum wagon _____
4. Ditty bags _____
5. Lead steer _____
6. Remuda _____

7. Redeemer _____

8. Comancheros _____

9. LaReunion _____

10. Coxey's Army _____

11. Kangaroo Court _____

12. Ferguson Forum _____

13. Freedmen's Bureau _____

14. Cottonclads _____

15. Salt Dome _____

16. Come And Take It _____

17. Juneteenth _____

18. Gusher _____

19. Hall of State _____

20. Headright _____

21. Mustang _____

22. Quarter horse _____

23. Hot Oil _____

24. Know Nothing _____

25. The *Lively* _____

26. Local Option _____

27. Longhorn _____

28. Maverick _____

29. Black Bean _____

30. Friendship _____

31. Nester _____

32. Filibuster _____

33. Old Three Hundred _____

34. Prohibition _____

35. Obnoxious Acts _____

36. Semi-Colon Court _____

37. Runaway Scrape _____

38. "Twin Sisters" _____

39. Santa Rita _____

40. Santa Gertrudis _____

41. Six-shooter _____

42. Stetson _____

43. Sunday House _____

44. Texas Deck _____

45. Texas Fever _____

46. Texas 40 and 8 _____

47. Bracero _____

48. Wetback _____

49. Chicano _____

50. Drummer Tax _____

For a change of pace, define the following "foreign" terms:

51. *Adelsverein* _____

52. *Alcalde* _____

53. *Amigo* _____

54. *Ayuntamiento* _____

55. *Cabildo* _____

56. *La Bahia* _____

57. *Peyote* _____

58. *Pueblo* _____

59. *Rodeo* _____

60. *Vara* _____

Identify the following acronyms that you are likely to encounter in any conversation with Texans or other Americans.

61. AAUW _____

62. AF of L _____

63. UDC _____

64. DRT _____

65. DAR _____

66. SRT _____
67. SCV _____
68. GTT _____
69. JA _____
70. 6666 _____
71. OSR _____
72. LIT _____
73. CIO _____
74. IOCW _____
75. LULAC _____
76. UIL _____
77. MAYO _____
78. TEA _____
79. XIT _____
80. MSC _____

Continue by defining some "nicknames," or references to folks and things.

81. The Alamo _____
82. Babe of the Alamo _____
83. Architect of Annexation _____
84. Father of Texas _____
85. The Last Democrat _____
86. Swamp Fox of the Sulphur _____
87. Bet-A-Million Gates _____
88. Law West Of The Pecos _____
89. Billy The Kid _____
90. Big Foot _____
91. Horse Marines _____
92. Rio de los Palmos _____
93. Jinglebob John _____
94. Big D _____
95. Town Without a Toothache _____

96. Savior Of The Alamo _____
97. Add-Ran College _____
98. Duke of Duval _____
99. Black Stephen _____
100. Farmer Jim _____
101. RIP _____
102. Mina _____
103. Lexington of The Texas Revolution _____
104. Winchester Quarantine _____
105. The Raven _____
106. Bayou City _____
107. Dad _____
108. Father of Texas Education _____
109. Llano Estacado _____
110. Leadbelly _____
111. Mother of Texas _____
112. Magee Bend Dam _____
113. Mr. Speaker _____
114. Prince John _____
115. John O. Meusebach _____
116. Muldoon Catholic _____
117. O. Henry _____
118. O.P.Q. _____
119. Ringtail Panther _____
120. Shanghai _____
121. Deaf _____
122. The Mighty T _____
123. Betsy Ross of Texas _____
124. Three Legged Willie _____
125. Astrodome _____
126. Philip Hendrik Nering Bogel _____
127. "Ma" _____
128. "Pa" _____
129. Cactus Jack _____

130. Old Gray Fox _____
131. Landslide Lyndon _____
132. Judy Garland of Rock; Hippie Queen of Show
     Business _____
133. King of Ragtime _____
134. Cowboy Congressman _____
135. Pappy _____
136. Cradle of Western Swing _____
137. Lost Battalion _____
138. Alfalfa Bill _____
139. Texas Jack _____
140. Pole-Cat _____
141. The Singing Brakeman _____
142. Sissy _____
143. Dirty Thirty _____
144. The Old Scotsman _____
145. Voice of the Southwest Conference _____
146. Yellow Rose of Texas _____
147. The Old Alcalde _____
148. Veto Governor of Texas _____
149. Fastest Man Alive and Bullet Bob _____
150. America's Team _____

Answers

1. Mostly northerners who invaded southern states in the wake of the Civil War to take advantage of economic and political opportunities that abounded in the chaos of the defeated states.
2. Native southerners who collaborated with Carpetbaggers and other Radicals to take advantage of those same economic and political opportunities.
3. Wagon provided for drovers on post-Civil War cattle drives to store their personal belongings.
4. Several meanings: first, bags containing personal belongings of drovers stored on the "hoodlum wagon"; second, small bags for gentlemen's toilet articles; third and more recently, "care" packages prepared by the patriotic for service men and women, especially those stationed overseas.
5. Anyone who is a habitual leader; specifically, an animal that just naturally finds its way to the head of the herd on a cattle drive. Sometimes such animals would be retained so they could be the "lead steer" on the next drive. Has applications to other things than cattle drives, however.
6. The herd of horses maintained for working cattle on a ranch or on a cattle drive. Each cowboy or drover had a "string" of horses in the remuda that he alone rode, although usually he did not own the animals.
7. Texas Democrats who reclaimed political control of their former Confederate state from Carpetbaggers, Scalawags, and Radical Republicans.
8. Indian traders who dealt with Plains Indians, usually in stolen goods, which they then infused into the legitimate Santa Fe Trail trade. Mostly they

operated out of New Mexico and into the Panhandle and far West Texas.

9. Socialist commune established near Dallas in 1854; later the name of that onion bulb in Dallas.

10. In days gone by, any large family feast was said to be adequate to "feed Coxey's army." It is a specific reference to men led by Lewis G. Fry from Los Angeles across Texas in 1894 to join Jacob S. Coxey's "army" of the unemployed who marched on Washington for job relief during the Panic of 1893.

11. Any extra-legal proceeding; specifically, what Governor James E. Ferguson called the state legislature that impeached him in 1918.

12. Publication of Governor James E. Ferguson, who dominated state politics from 1915 to the mid-1930s; large-scale advertisers in the publication, it was charged, often received lucrative state contracts.

13. Federal relief agency that operated in Texas and other former Confederate states after the Civil War to assist the freedmen and women to adjust to their new status, although at the time they had not been declared citizens by the Fourteenth Amendment. The agency monitored labor contracts, distributed rations to displaced freedmen, and established schools, among other things.

14. When General John B. Magruder recaptured Galveston from Federal troops in September 1862, some of his men arrived at the battle aboard flat-bottomed riverboats with cotton bales on the decks for cover—hence, "cottonclads."

15. Natural geologic formations created by salt rising

through the strata that form "pools" in which crude oil collects. These were good drilling sites in the early days of the oil industry in Texas.

16. The message painted on their flag by defenders of a cannon in Gonzales in October 1835. It was intended to inform Mexican soldiers that the cannon would not be surrendered peacefully.

17. General Gordon Granger arrived in Galveston on June 19, 1865, and declared the Civil War over in Texas. Since that date, Texas blacks have regarded it as their unique day of independence from slavery.

18. An oil well that "blows in." Pressure released by natural gas heaves oil into the air with great force when the drill penetrates a pool of crude. It was a somewhat common occurrence in the early days of drilling but later quite rare because of the development of methods to control the pressure.

19. Exhibition hall on the state fair grounds in Dallas; constructed for the 1936 Texas Centennial exhibition at a cost of $1.2 million; later a museum operated by the Dallas Historical Society.

20. In the early days of Texas settlement, the Mexican government—and later the Republic—offered land as an inducement to settlement. A "headright" amounted to 640 acres of the public domain available for a pledge of development. In addition, the Republic's congress offered for a time "bounty grants" of 320 acres for each three months service in its army.

21. Generally a wild horse that once ranged in herds in Texas; from the Spanish *mesta* (stockraisers) and *mesteños* (mustangs).

22. A mixture of English and Spanish breeds trained to

race for a quarter of a mile; noted for stamina and bursts of speed for short distances, thus a good animal for working cattle.

23. Oil produced in excess of the Railroad Commission's quota for each well; a major problem in the EasTex Field during 1930s when overproduction forced the price of crude oil downward.

24. Reference to members of the American Party, a secretive nativist group active in Texas politics in the 1850s. Its members would respond that they "knew nothing" about it when asked.

25. The ship *Lively* brought the first colonists to Stephen F. Austin's colony in 1821.

26. Occasionally the state legislature will leave questions such as liquor sales, horse racing, some sales taxes, etc., to be decided by lesser jurisdictions, usually counties or cities.

27. Longhorns originally referred to the tough, hybrid cattle that resulted from unselective breeding among wild herds; later a specific breed, and also the mascot of the University of Texas athletic teams.

28. Specifically, an unbranded cow, allegedly so named because Samuel A. Maverick—without much concern for rightful ownership—built his herd by claiming animals not previously marked.

29. "Drawing the black bean" is a reference to receiving any sort of unwanted duty. It is also a reference to the method by which it was determined who among the Mier Expedition captives would be executed in 1842 when their punishment for violating Mexican territory was decimation—the men drew beans from a hat in

which ninety percent were white, ten percent black.

30. The state motto, based upon the alleged meaning of the Indian word, *Tejas*.

31. A nester is a frontier settler, especially a farmer, who built his "nest" on range formerly utilized by cattlemen.

32. "Filibuster" has several meanings, among them: leaders of illegal invasions of Texas during the days of Spanish control, especially Philip Nolan, Augustus Magee and Bernardo Gutierrez de Lara, and Dr. James Long, who attempted to seize some or all of Texas from Spanish control (Nolan did not, but was suspected of it); and later a description of those who attempted similar missions in Mexico and Central American countries.

33. Stephen F. Austin was authorized to settle 300 families on his original empresarial grant. Scholars think he actually settled only 297 families in the initial phase, but they are known by this reference anyway.

34. "Prohibition" means prohibiting the production, distribution, and consumption of beverages containing alcohol. It was the most pervasive political issue in Texas from 1875 until 1915, the subject of the Eighteenth Amendment to the U.S. Constitution, and a matter of various "local options" for Texas counties, cities, and even precincts.

35. "Obnoxious" was what Texas Democrats called the legislative program of Governor Edmund J. Davis during Reconstruction. The Obnoxious Acts gave the governor significantly greater power than the

office had enjoyed previously, and such powers were removed by the Constitution of 1876.

36. "Semi-Colon Court" was the name applied to the Texas Supreme Court that ruled in favor of Governor Edmund J. Davis' claim that the election of 1873 was illegal. The court did so on the basis of punctuation in Section 6, Article 3, of the Constitution of 1869.

37. The flight of citizens before Santa Anna's armies during the Texas Revolution in the spring of 1836.

38. The "Twin Sisters" were two small cannon sent by the citizens of Cincinnati for the Texans to use during the revolution against Mexico.

39. The oil well discovered in 1923 on land reserved for the University of Texas that has provided a significant portion of that institution's endowment. It is also shared by Texas A&M.

40. Santa Gertrudis was the land grant that became the King Ranch in South Texas; also, a breed of cattle developed there by Robert Kleberg from short-horn and Brahman stock.

41. A six-shooter is a revolver, a hand-held weapon capable of firing six bullets when its cylinder "revolves" with each pull of the trigger. Its use made lethal violence more frequent on the Texas frontier. Also used to describe the Colt revolver, the first of many varieties of revolvers to reach Texas.

42. The hats manufactured and marketed by the John B. Stetson Hat Company of Philadelphia. The "Badge of a Texan" is broad-brimmed to protect the wearer from sun, wind, and rain.

43. Residences in town, especially in German communities, of rural farmers who came to town

on Saturday for market and stayed over to attend
church on Sunday.

44. The uppermost deck of a river steamboat.

45. Bovine disease carried by parasitic ticks. It was
    carried up the cattle trails and infected domestic
    stock along the way.

46. Reference to practice during World War I of
    shipping men or mules in quantities of forty men
    or eight mules to the railroad car. Later a veteran's
    organization adopted the term for its name. Many
    Texans were members.

47. A bracero is a migrant worker from Mexico who
    came to Texas (and other states) to work in
    truck-farming operations. Braceros are (or were)
    legal workers, but the term is often used in place
    of "wetback."

48. Reference, usually pejorative, to illegal migrants
    from Mexico and later from other Latin American
    countries.

49. Chicano became a popular and sometimes
    preferred reference to Mexican Americans during
    the 1960s. When used by Mexican-Americans, it
    was intended to express pride in cultural heritage.

50. Governor Oran Roberts wanted to enhance state
    revenue with this levy on traveling salesmen, or
    "drummers," who did business in the state,
    especially by traveling on railroads constructed
    with public subsidies; later declared
    unconstitutional.

51. The *Adelsverein* (Association of Noblemen), or
    Meinzer Verein, relocated German immigrants to
    Texas and assisted them in obtaining land and
    becoming established once they arrived.

52. In the Spanish governmental system, the *alcalde*

was a municipal leader similar to a mayor. Some judicial functions also accompanied the office.

53. Term for "friend."

54. Under Spanish government, the local town council.

55. The *cabildo* was the building in which the *ayuntamiento*, or town council, met; hence, "city hall."

56. *La Bahia*, or "the bay," generally refers to La Bahia del Espiritu Santo, located near Matagorda Bay.

57. Peyote is a small, spineless cactus with narcotic properties; used by some Indians in religious rites and by others to induce intoxication.

58. A *pueblo* is a town with an official charter, or recognized local government.

59. Pronounced "Ro-dee-o" in Texas, but sometimes "Ro-day-o" elsewhere, the word refers to competition among cowboys (and cowgirls) in events utilizing skills associated with working cattle, such as riding bucking horses, calf-roping, etc. Today rodeo includes such non-traditional events as bull riding and barrel racing.

60. Under the Spanish system, a *vara* is a surveyor's unit of land measurement; one *vara* equals 33 and 1/3 inches.

61. American Association of University Women, an organization of women who hold baccalaureate or higher degrees that seeks to advance the educational opportunities for women.

62. American Federation of Labor, the union for skilled craftsmen.

63. United Daughters of the Confederacy, an organization of female descendants of persons who served the Confederacy.

64. Daughters of the Republic of Texas, an organization

of female descendants of anyone who lived in Texas during the time of the Republic. The DRT plays a strong role in preserving the memory of that era and, as custodians of the Alamo, the crucible of Texas history.

65. Daughters of the American Revolution, an organization of descendants of participants in the American Revolution.

66. Sons of the Republic of Texas, an organization of male descendants of persons who lived in Texas during the time of the Republic.

67. Sons of Confederate Veterans, an organization of descendants of those who served the Confederacy.

68. "Gone To Texas," or how some modern Texans became eligible for membership in the DRT and the SRT—their ancestors left some previous residence and made their way to Texas, often leaving behind the acronym "GTT" on tax records and cabin doors as sufficient communication about their destination and determination to make the move permanent.

69. JA, the initials of John Adair; became the recognized brand of Adair and partner Charles Goodnight for livestock belonging to their ranch in Palo Duro Canyon late in the nineteenth century.

70. 6666, the registered brand of Samuel Burk Burnett's ranch in the Wichita Falls area. Popular culture maintains that the name was derived from the poker hand that won the ranch.

71. OSR signifies Old San Antonio Road, which is the same as the Old Nacogdoches Road if one happens to be in San Antonio. The road was begun in 1691 by Domingo Terán de los Rios, first provincial governor of Texas, for access to Mission San

Francisco de los Tejas in East Texas. Also known as El Camino Real and by several other names.

72. Identification brand of the LIT Ranch, founded in 1877 and owned by George W. Littlefield.

73. Congress of Industrial Organizations, a labor union organized on the basis of specific industries; originally the Committee for Industrial Organizations when a part of the American Federation of Labor.

74. International Oil and Chemical Workers, a union of workers in those related industries.

75. League of United Latin American Citizens, organized on April 17, 1929, in San Antonio.

76. University Interscholastic League. Started in 1910, the UIL oversees competitions—both athletic and academic—among Texas school students in more than fifty activities.

77. Mexican American Youth Organization, founded in San Antonio in 1967.

78. Texas Education Agency, founded in 1950, is the state agency charged with establishing standards for public education.

79. Famed Panhandle ranch, established in 1885 on land allocated as payment for building the state capitol in Austin.

80. Manned Spacecraft Center, established in 1961 near Houston. It is the control center for all manned space activities under the National Aeronautics and Space Administration (NASA); renamed the Lyndon B. Johnson Space Center in 1973.

81. Mission San Antonio de Valero, established in 1718.

82. Angelina Dickenson, daughter of Captain Almaron

Dickenson, artillery commander at the Alamo, and Suzanna A. Wilkinson Dickenson.

83. President Anson Jones, third president of the Republic of Texas, who was in office when Texas became the twenty-eighth state of the American Union.

84. Stephen Fuller Austin, who, beginning in 1821, was the first *empresario* to introduce legal American settlers in Texas. He also served Texas as its primary representative to successive Mexican governments in the 1820s and 1830s, as the first commander of its military force, representative to the United States, and secretary of state of the Republic.

85. Senator Joseph Weldon Bailey; a Bourbon Democrat whose political career survived into the Progressive Era despite his being out of step with the times.

86. Cullen Montgomery Baker, a Robin Hood-type outlaw during the Reconstruction period.

87. John W. Gates, barbed-wire salesman without equal who earned his nickname by betting stockmen that his product would contain their animals; later a railroad builder and entrepreneur.

88. "Judge" Roy Bean, who established residence in the area west of the Pecos River about 1882, and from his bench at Langtry ruled on legal statutes with highly personal interpretations.

89. William Bonney, youthful gunman who operated in various places in the West, including West Texas.

90. William Alexander Anderson Wallace, a man of large physical proportions and legendary frontier feats (no pun intended), who, among other things, survived the Black Bean Incident.

91. Command of Mounted Rangers in the Texas

Revolution led by Isaac Burton; they earned this nickname by capturing several Mexican ships in Copano Bay.

92. First reference to the Rio Grande.

93. John Simpson Chisum, West Texas and New Mexico rancher named for "jinglebob," or loose-hanging earmark on his stock.

94. Dallas, my-o-yes, as in "Big D, little a, double-l-a-s."

95. Reference to Hereford, Deaf Smith County, where the natural presence of fluorine protects residents from tooth decay.

96. Clara Driscoll, who bought a thirty-day option on the remains of the Alamo in 1903, then held it against all challengers; president-general of the Daughters of the Republic of Texas, custodians of the Alamo.

97. Addison and Randolph Clark were the founders of a college located at Thorp Spring that evolved into Texas Christian University, now located in Fort Worth.

98. The original Duke was Archer (Archie) Parr, who served in the state senate for twenty years; his son, George Berham Parr is a better-known Duke of Duval (County) to Texans familiar with the U.S. Senate race of 1948, when Parr "delivered" the votes that elected Lyndon B. Johnson over Coke R. Stevenson by a state-wide margin of only eighty-seven votes.

99. Estavanico, or Stephen the Moor, accompanied Alvar Nuñez Cabeza de Vaca during their captivity among Texas Indians in the 1520s.

100. Governor James E. Ferguson, who earned the nickname in the campaign of 1914 by

concentrating on Texas' largely rural electorate; he promised farmers various kinds of relief, including a tenant-rent law.

101. RIP became the nickname of John Salmon Ford, Ranger and Civil War commander who always concluded reports with RIP, for "Rest In Peace," when reporting casualties, and in Ford's command there usually were casualties.

102. Previous name (1834–1837) for the city of Bastrop. After Francisco Xavier Mina.

103. Reference to the Battle of Gonzales, fought on October 2, 1835, between Texans who defended a cannon and Mexican troops ordered to confiscate it; regarded as the beginning of the military phase of the Texas Revolution.

104. Charles Goodnight proclaimed the "Winchester Quarantine" at his JA Ranch to prevent trail herds from coming in to consume water and grass and possibly to spread bovine disease.

105. Reference to Sam Houston, a name given to him by Cherokees, who adopted him and with whom he resided at various times.

106. Houston is known as the Bayou City from its location on Buffalo Bayou.

107. Columbus Marvin ("Dad") Joiner, discoverer of the EasTex Oil Field, October 1930.

108. President Mirabeau B. Lamar earned this nickname because of his advocacy of education, especially of a university, during his administration as president of the Republic of Texas.

109. Llano Estacado, or Staked Plains, the "high plateau extending from the central western part of Texas northward over most of the Panhandle of

Texas and westward into eastern New Mexico" (*Handbook of Texas,* vol. 2, p. 69).

110. Huddie Leadbetter, blues composer and performer who resided for a while in the Texas penitentiary.

111. Jane Herbert Wilkinson Long, wife of Dr. James Long, who accompanied her husband on his second trip to Texas; she survived, he did not, and for her pioneering earned the nickname of "Mother of Texas" (it being necessary to get someone for the title since Stephen F. Austin, the "Father of Texas," remained a bachelor).

112. Magee Bend Dam was the original name for the Sam Rayburn Reservoir in East Texas. It was renamed for Rayburn in gratitude for his assistance in obtaining appropriations for the project.

113. Samuel Taliaferro Rayburn, Speaker of the U.S. House of Representatives longer than any other. According to a television report during the 1960 Democratic convention in Los Angeles, Kennedy forces had assigned Rayburn quarters away from the headquarters hotel. The speaker was quoted after surveying his rooms, "I am an old man of considerable power, and I will not stay in this dump." He didn't; room was made for him at the headquarters hotel.

114. General John Bankhead Magruder, commander in Texas during the Civil War (1862–1865), in recognition of his theatrical flair.

115. John O. Meusebach is the assumed, Americanized name of Ottfried, Hans Freiherr von Meusebach, German nobleman and leader of German immigrants to Texas. In 1845 he relinquished the title to become a Texas citizen.

116. Reference to an insincere baptism into the Catholic

Church during colonial days when such was required to be admitted to Texas and to receive land grants; in honor of Father Michael Muldoon, who was said to perform many such baptisms.

117. Nom de plume of William Sydney Porter, famed short-story writer, bank teller, and for a time, resident of the state penitentiary.

118. Signature on otherwise anonymous letters from Anthony Butler, "secret" agent, that were intended to incite Texas colonists against Mexico.

119. Nickname of Martin Palmer, participant in the Fredonia Rebellion and a signer of the Texas Declaration of Independence.

120. Abel Head Pierce, Texas cattleman.

121. Erastus ("Deaf") Smith, Sam Houston's chief scout during the San Jacinto campaign.

122. The battleship *USS Texas*. After service in both World Wars, The "Mighty T" was retired to museum duty and is now berthed at San Jacinto.

123. Johanna Troutman made a flag for a Georgia battalion commanded by Colonel William Ward as they prepared to heed the call for aid during the Texas Revolution. Troutman's flag was white silk with a blue, five-pointed star and contained the words "Liberty or Death." It was called the Flag of the Lone Star, and was torn to shreds when the unit, then serving under the command of James Fannin at Goliad, was captured.

124. Robert McAlpin Williamson, lawyer, activist in the Texas Revolution, and Supreme Court justice during the period of the Republic. Williamson's right leg was drawn back at the knee, so he wore a wooden leg strapped to his knee for support—hence, Three Legged Willie.

125. The real name for this "Eighth Wonder of the World" is the Harris County Domed Stadium. It is located in Houston and is the site of home games for the Houston Astros baseball team and the Houston Oilers football team.

126. This fellow is better known in Texas history as the Baron de Bastrop, the man who vouched for Moses Austin when Austin made his first request for an empresarial grant, and who later served as the government's land agent for the grant administered by Stephen F. Austin.

127. Miriam Amanda ("Ma") Ferguson, wife of Governor James E. Ferguson, and governor in her own right (1925–1927 and 1933–1935); nickname resulted from her initials.

128. When Miriam Amanda Ferguson became "Ma," "Farmer Jim" Ferguson was given the nickname of "Pa."

129. John Nance Garner of Uvalde, speaker of the United States House of Representatives and vice president of the United States during the first two administrations of President Franklin D. Roosevelt. When called by Lyndon B. Johnson for advice on whether or not LBJ should accept John F. Kennedy's invitation to join him on the Democratic ticket in 1960, Garner said, "Lyndon, the vice presidency ain't worth a pitcher of warm spit," or so it was reported.

130. Oscar Fitzallen Holcombe, long-time mayor of Houston.

131. In 1948, Lyndon B. Johnson defeated Coke R. Stevenson for a seat in the U.S. Senate by a total of eighty-seven votes in the statewide race. The name was used mostly in Texas until Republican

presidential candidate Barry Goldwater popularized it nationally in their race in 1964, which Lyndon won by a landslide.

132. This lady from Port Arthur earned two nicknames before a drug overdose and hard living ended her life—Janis Joplin.

133. Scott Joplin, born in Texarkana, noted composer of "ragged time" music.

134. Richard Mifflin Kleberg, member of the family who owns the King Ranch and U.S. congressman (1931–1945) who brought Lyndon B. Johnson to Washington as an aide.

135. Wilbert (W.) Lee O'Daniel, flour salesman-become-governor (1939-1941) who gained fame on a state-wide radio show during the 1930s. His radio show's theme song, "Pass The Biscuits, Pappy," earned him this nickname.

136. Reference to Fort Worth because the Light Crust Dough Boys, and especially Bob Wills, played there during the development of this genre of music.

137. 2nd Battalion, 131st Field Artillery Regiment, 36th Infantry Division, captured by Japanese in Java on March 10, 1942. They spent forty-two months in military prisons from Singapore to Manchuria until liberated in 1945. Pierre Boulle's *Bridge On The River Kwai* described some of their imprisonment and activities. Called "Lost Battalion" because the U.S. government refused to release any information about their fate.

138. William Henry Murray, born in Toadsuck, Texas, but governor of Oklahoma in the 1930s; earned name from farm lectures on the merits of alfalfa.

139. John Burrell Omohundro, cowboy, Confederate soldier, cattle trail driver, co-star with William F.

("Buffalo Bill") Cody in "Scouts Of The Prairie"—the original Wild West Show, and dime-novel subject.

140. Name used by Texas Confederate soldiers to describe their commander, French nobleman Camille Arman de Jules Marce, Prince de Polignac. The troops found the proper name a mouthful.

141. Jimmie (James Charles) Rodgers, perhaps the first genuine "country" music recording artist. Although from Mississippi, Rodgers lived his final years in the Hill Country combating tuberculosis.

142. Frances Farenthold, liberal legislator and gubernatorial candidate for the Democratic nomination in 1972.

143. Coalition of members of the Texas House of Representatives, some liberal and some conservative, who opposed the way Speaker Gus Mutscher ran the House in the 1971 session.

144. Gordon McClendon, the voice of the Mutual Radio Network.

145. Kern Tips, who did play-by-play broadcasts of Southwest Conference football games on the Humble network for thirty-two years.

146. Reference (in legend) to Emily Morgan, the mulatto with whom Santa Anna allegedly dallied while Sam Houston's men charged during the Battle of San Jacinto.

147. Governor Oran Roberts, who held many offices besides that one, including presiding at the Texas secession convention and at a constitutional convention, justice of the state supreme court, and senator-elect (who didn't get to serve.)

148. Governor Dan Moody, who vetoed fifteen bills during the regular session of the legislature (only

one was overridden) and 102 bills after the session concluded.

149. Pass receiver Bob Hayes, who played with the Dallas Cowboys; Hayes' speed made him an excellent pass receiver.

150. This nickname was first applied to the Dallas Cowboys, although some players and fans regretted it—especially when it motivated opposing teams to greater efforts.

9

How Well Did I Do?: Scoring

Normally, academic grades go something like this: ninety percent for an "A," eighty percent for a "B" and so on, with sixty percent considered passing. There are about 1000 questions in this book, not counting about a dozen or so "Bonus" questions or the "Diagnostic Quiz." If you are keeping close score, don't worry about missing the Bonus questions, but give yourself credit if you knew them.

Ninety percent for an "A" would require 900 correct answers; eighty percent for a "B" would require 800 correct answers; seventy percent for a "C" would require 700 correct answers; and sixty percent for "passing" would require 600 correct answers. That is standard university fare, but probably too much to expect for folks who may have been out the academic game for a while.

Look at it this way. When students graduate with a baccalaureate degree at Stephen F. Austin State University, the vice president certifies the candidates to the president by saying they are "persons of understanding." If they are candidates for a master's degree, they are persons of "reason," and persons of "wisdom" if they receive a doctorate. Let's say that you are a "person of understanding" if you scored at least 300 on the total examination; however, there is a lot more you could understand about Texas. You are a "person of reason" if you scored 500 points on the total exam, and a "person of wisdom" if you scored more than 700 points.

But the "score" is important only to you. If you do not know as much as you would like to know about Texas, then learn more. I hope a good place to start is in the answer sections of these quizzes. That is the point of running them within each chapter, close to the questions. The answer sections will give you information that is required to respond to the questions, and they are a good place to begin to learn more. But they are only a beginning.